Ezra, Nehemiah,
and Esther

Westminster Bible Companion

Series Editors

Patrick D. Miller

David L. Bartlett

Ezra, Nehemiah, and Esther

JOHANNA W. H. VAN WIJK-BOS

Westminster John Knox Press
Louisville, Kentucky

Book design by Publishers' WorkGroup
Cover design by Drew Stevens

First Edition

Published by Westminster John Knox Press
Louisville, Kentucky

This book is printed on acid-free paper that meets the American National Standards Institute Z39.48 standard. ♾

PRINTED IN THE UNITED STATES OF AMERICA

98 99 00 01 02 03 04 05 06 07 — 10 9 8 7 6 5 4 3 2 1

Library of Congress Cataloging-in-Publication Data

van Wijk-Bos, Johanna W. H., date.
    Ezra, Nehemiah, and Esther / Johanna W.H. van Wijk-Bos. — 1st ed.
        p.   cm. — (Westminster Bible Companion)
    ISBN 0-664-25597-3 (alk. paper)
    1. Bible. O.T. Ezra—Commentaries. 2. Bible. O.T. Nehemiah—Commentaries. 3. Bible. O.T. Esther—Commentaries. I. Title. II. Series.
BS1355.3.V36   1998
222—dc21   97-41415

Contents

Series Foreword

This series of study guides to the Bible is offered to the church and more specifically to the laity. In daily devotions, in church school classes, and in listening to the preached word, individual Christians turn to the Bible for a sustaining word, a challenging word, and a sense of direction. The word that scripture brings may be highly personal as one deals with the demands and surprises, the joys and sorrows, of daily life. It also may have broader dimensions as people wrestle with moral and theological issues that involve us all. In every congregation and denomination, controversies arise that send ministry and laity alike back to the Word of God to find direction for dealing with difficult matters that confront us.

A significant number of lay women and men in the church also find themselves called to the service of teaching. Most of the time they will be teaching the Bible. In many churches, the primary sustained attention to the Bible and the discovery of its riches for our lives have come from the ongoing teaching of the Bible by persons who have not engaged in formal theological education. They have been willing, and often eager, to study the Bible in order to help others drink from its living water.

This volume is part of a series of books, the Westminster Bible Companion, intended to help the laity of the church read the Bible more clearly and intelligently. Whether such reading is for personal direction or for the teaching of others, the reader cannot avoid the difficulties of trying to understand these words from long ago. The scriptures are clear and clearly available to everyone as they call us to faith in the God who is revealed in Jesus Christ and as they offer to every human being the word of salvation. No companion volumes are necessary in order to hear such words truly. Yet every reader of scripture who pauses to ponder and think further about any text has questions that are not immediately answerable simply by reading the text of scripture. Such questions may be about historical and geographical details or about words that are obscure or so loaded with meaning that one cannot tell at a glance what is at stake. They may be about the fundamental meaning of a passage or about what connection a particular text might have to our contemporary world. Or a teacher preparing for a church school class may simply want to know: What should I say about this biblical passage when I have to teach it next Sunday? It is our hope that these volumes, written by teachers and pastors with long experience studying and teaching the Bible in the church, will help members of the church who want and need to study the Bible with their questions.

The New Revised Standard Version of the Bible is the basis for the interpretive comments that each author provides. The NRSV text is presented at the beginning of the discussion so that the reader may have at hand in a single volume both the scripture passage and the exposition of its meaning. In some instances, where inclusion of the entire passage is not necessary for understanding either the text or the interpreter's discussion, the presentation of the NRSV text may be abbreviated. Usually, the whole of the biblical text is given.

We hope this series will serve the community of faith, opening the Word of God to all the people, so that they may be sustained and guided by it.

Ezra-Nehemiah

Introduction

WHY EZRA AND NEHEMIAH?

Have you ever sat down and read through the books of Ezra and Nehemiah? When did you last hear a sermon on a text from these two? Who were they exactly? What did they do? When did they live? What is the story? My guess is that we have rarely heard these texts used in preaching, that we may have tried to read them through but became stuck at one point, and that we know in fact very little about either Ezra or Nehemiah.

Our ignorance need not embarrass us, for we are probably in a large company. Yet our absence of familiarity with this material is to our loss. Ezra and Nehemiah deal with a crucial period of the history of the biblical community. Without the efforts made here and the reorientation of the community that took place, Judaism might never have been, nor Christianity. In the stories and documents, the speeches and lists of Ezra and Nehemiah, we may view the roots of much that is familiar to Christians in their community. It is essential to study the shape and formation of our roots so we may understand ourselves better. Moreover, we may find a message here of God's faithfulness with the covenant community. First with the ancient covenant community that gave birth to both Judaism and Christianity. In that faithfulness we may find comfort and look to God's ongoing presence in the midst of our own confusion and struggle for survival.

At least a part of the reason for our ignorance may reside in the material found in these books. A good deal of the Ezra-Nehemiah text strikes one as confusing and repetitive. There are chapters that consist only of lists of names, not most people's favorite reading. The story does not seem to be able to settle on a specific period of time. Three Persian kings are mentioned as if they all lived at the same period, whereas in fact their reigns spanned more than a century. Did Ezra come first, to be followed by Nehemiah? Why then does Ezra pop up in the middle of the book named

for Nehemiah (Nehemiah 8—9), and why are both of them present at the
grand celebration of the city wall dedication (Neh. 12:33)? If the two of
them were around at the same time, when exactly was that?

In the course of our exploration, we may find answers to some of these
questions. At other times, we may find unexpected insights when we refo-
cus our view. At all times, we hope to become better acquainted with these
books and learn from them, as they may instruct us in our time.

Many students of Ezra and Nehemiah believe that these texts were originally one book and should be approached as if they were. The two books
are indeed concerned with the same issues during approximately the same
period of time; therefore I present one introduction for both. Because the
books are named after two figures, we might expect these to be in the foreground of the picture. To some extent, this is indeed so. Both Ezra and
Nehemiah play prominent roles, especially as they appear in their own accounts. On the other hand, when we focus on them closely, their contours
become blurred, and they tend to disappear into their time and their community. First, we will consider the context, the time, and the place into
which we can set the events recounted here. Then we will review the different groups of people that occur in the text. Last, we contemplate Ezra
and Nehemiah, the possible authorship and the theology of the books.

THE TIME

The events reflected in these biblical books took place over a long period of
time, a far longer period than two individual lifetimes could span. Three Persian kings are mentioned as one person in Ezra 6:14: "They finished their
building by command of the God of Israel and by decree of Cyrus, Darius,
and Artaxerxes, king of Persia." The translators of the Bible found the mention of three kings who are counted as one "king of Persia" so confusing that
they put the word *king* in front of Artaxerxes: "king Artaxerxes of Persia." But
the Aramaic original boldly refers to the three rulers of Persia as one king. In
our context, it would be as if someone mentioned George Washington, Abraham Lincoln, and John F. Kennedy as one president of the United States. We
would be quick to correct such a misrepresentation of the facts. A fourth ruler
who appears is Ahasuerus (Ezra 4) and perhaps a fifth with Artaxerxes, since
there were at least two Persian kings by that name. None of these kings are
assigned to specific time periods. What is going on? Is there accidental confusion, deliberate obfuscation? I suggest that the interest of Ezra-Nehemiah
is not in chronology. The writers were neither confused nor trying to con-

fuse others; they were not interested in exact dates but rather in the realities of their time. So we will try to follow their lead and not get lost in series of dates but take into account the period stretching roughly from 539 until 400 B.C.E. (Before Common Era, formerly designated B.C.).

What sort of times were they? One reality that is starkly present for the community of faith that is described here is the reality of Persia. All the kings mentioned in Ezra and Nehemiah are Persian kings; they are the overlords of the small province of the Persian realm to which the Jews had been allowed to return. Whether these kings lived in 520 or 420, the reality of foreign domination remained the same and carried some of the same implications at least. There were always taxes to be paid, and we will encounter this reality and its complications. There was always royal permission to be sought for every significant step taken; there were intrigues related to the court causing difficulties for one protagonist or another. Life was economically and physically unstable for most people in Judah. The situation was not the same as war, but it was the result and long aftermath of a war that devastated the country of Judah and its capital, Jerusalem, in the early part of the sixth century. Thereafter Judah was not to be independent again but became instead a vassal state to different empires that followed one another in that part of the world. The first of these empires was Persia, which was the ruling power from 539 until 332 B.C.E.

The first Persian ruler, Cyrus, is best known in a biblical context for having allowed the Judeans who had been taken in exile to Babylon to return home. This permission was given by royal decree, and with it the book of Ezra opens. From other contexts, Cyrus is known as an enlightened ruler who left the many peoples and ethnic groups incorporated into his realm to work out their own identity, allowing them to keep their customs, religious and otherwise. On the other hand, Cyrus was also a political and military leader interested in the stability of his realm, nervous about potential rebellion and zeal for independence on the part of vassal states, and in constant need of economic resources for his vast empire. What can be said of Cyrus we may safely assume for all the Persian kings after him. For the small city state of Judah, it may in these respects as well have been one king instead of three or four or five. It was not so much the particular character of a given ruler as the general character of the reality that mattered. The reality of the period for Judah was dependence on Persia, being overseen by outsiders, and being heavily taxed, a condition that, apart from being a hardship in itself, also lent itself easily to internal corruption.

Nevertheless, without the permission given by Cyrus and the aid he provided for the first return by the exiles to Judah, the opportunity for any kind of rebuilding and restoration would not have taken place. So the period and the material of Ezra-Nehemiah are under the banner of the decree given by Cyrus: "Any of those among you who are of his people . . . are now permitted to go up to Jerusalem in Judah" (Ezra 1:3). There were several "returns" from Persia to Judah. At least three of them are recorded in the Ezra-Nehemiah material. It is natural that such organized expeditions would have taken place more than once, with a steady trickle of smaller groups or individuals in between. It was, in any case, from these returnees, the "children of the exile," that the push came for the restoration of Jerusalem rather than from the remnants of the community that had continued to live there after the Babylonian conquest. That people had continued to live in Judah and Jerusalem and in the surrounding areas is another important reality of that time. There was tension between these groups and the returning exiles. In the province of Judah, the community of faith consisted of different groups with different interests. I will return to the tensions produced by this situation when we consider the people who cross the stage in Ezra and Nehemiah.

If the context of Ezra and Nehemiah was thus fraught with difficulties in a political and economic sense, from a religious perspective the situation was also far from ideal. The Babylonian Exile had robbed the ancient Israelite faith community of the most important guarantees of God's presence with it: the temple, the land, and the Davidic kingship. All these were devastated. Ezra and Nehemiah reflect the ongoing attempts to restore a sense of religious identity and stability to the community. The most obvious means to establish this goal were the rebuilding of the temple and instituting regular worship, as well as the rebuilding of the city itself. There is an ongoing concern in this material with the restoration of the "house of God." I suggest that we conceive of this structure in its widest possible sense and include in it the entire city with its restored walls as well as the rebuilt temple. A new temple and a rebuilt city would restore to the community a sense of itself and its relation to its God, and of God's presence with them. They were true restorations in the sense that old symbols and structures in this way found a new place and renewed significance for the people. At the same time, the priesthood rose to a place of importance it had not known before, since it took the place of the kingship that was gone. Priests thus play a very significant role in the Ezra-Nehemiah books. A rallying point that was certainly not entirely new but that took on new shape and importance at this time was the written law. Documents are significant signposts in these books, and of all of them the law of Moses is the most important. This attention to a book or rather a scroll marks a shift away from the direct inspired word of God as it had come to the community through the prophets. Written testimony had been around for a long time, but as of this period a text moves to the center of the faith of the Judahite community. Ezra's task as described in Ezra 7:1–26 was to implement the laws as he found them in "the law of Moses" (7:6 and 25–26), of which he was a skilled student. For this implementation he had the authority granted by the king of Persia. Nehemiah 7—10 describes a public reading, interpretation, and implementation of the law, there called the book, or scroll, of the law of Moses. From the lengthy quotations used in Nehemiah 9, it is clear that this scroll or set of scrolls represented some form of the first five books of what later became the Bible. In Hebrew these first five scrolls are called the Torah. In Ezra and Nehemiah the Torah has become the rallying point for the community of faith, and from that period on it became important to have one common text as a foundational document. The task of the scribe took on special significance, next to that of priest, as is evident from the text of Ezra-Nehemiah.

Three main events then stand at the center of these biblical books: restoration of the temple, rebuilding of the city and its walls, and restoration of the community by means of the interpretation and application of the Torah.

THE PLACE

Rather than one place, there are a number of important locations in Ezra-Nehemiah. The action and movement in these books can be seen to go from one place to another: from Persia to Judah; from Babylon to Jerusalem; from exile to the house of God. There is a drive toward the one place— Jerusalem. Besides Jerusalem there are also the surrounding areas, the towns into which the exiles settle; there is "the land," and there is Samaria. But all of these are shot through with potential difficulties, even with hostility, and the pull is toward the city. Jerusalem stands in the center of the story that is told here. It is the point to which Babylon is the counterpoint. Jerusalem is from the start presented as the place where the God of the community is: "the God who is in Jerusalem" (Ezra 1:3). On the one hand, this expression may sound like the somewhat naive notion of the God of Israel one might expect from an outsider; on the other hand, this phrase gets directly at what was at stake for the people. In going to Judah, to Jerusalem, in returning home, they were also returning to the place that above all symbolized God's presence to them.

Zion, or Jerusalem, was for the exiles also a geographical location, a faraway home they had lost. But above all it was the place of God's presence. In the psalms, Zion is called a city with God in its midst (Ps. 46:4–5); it is said to be "God's holy mountain, . . . the joy of all the earth" (Ps. 48:1) and in one extravagant outburst is equated with God: "This is God, our God forever and ever" (Ps. 48:14). While this may be poetic exaggeration, it is also a witness to the power of this city over the religious imagination of the time.

The place that more than any symbolized God's presence within the city was the center of worship of ancient Israel—the temple. Where Jerusalem/ Zion takes on the characteristics I quoted above, it is as an extension of the temple. As such, as symbol and concrete sign of God's presence in the midst of the people, the temple and the city were thought of as holy, and they were to bring into existence God's vision for the creation and for God's people. The temple and Zion/Jerusalem also called into being the vision of what it meant to be God's community. Jerusalem was also the place of hope. In looking to Zion, the exiles looked to the vision of the community as God had called it into being, where love and justice walk hand in hand. It is to that place, the house of the God of Israel, that the exiles were called to return, to become a new household. It is that place which was devastated, and which needed rebuilding so the community could literally once more find a home in it.

A brief glance at the book of Lamentations makes clear how deeply the loss of city and temple affected the community. "Is it nothing to you, all you who pass by?" the poet cries,

> "Look and see
> if there is any sorrow like my sorrow,
>   which was brought upon me,
> which the LORD inflicted
>   on the day of his fierce anger."
> (Lam. 1:12)

Not only were the city and the temple devastated; this disaster had come upon the community, to its own understanding, as a punishment from God. The community that did not live up to the vision God had for it suffered the consequences.

In contrast to the ruin that Jerusalem/Zion had become, Babylon was a thriving, fertile city. Babylon was beautiful and powerful, the image of success. Without Babylon and its power, Jerusalem could not be rebuilt, and the exiles could not return there. There was no longer a king in Jerusalem, but there was one in Babylon, and it is by his word that events are set in motion, that they are halted and begin again. It is remarkable that in the midst of reports of hostilities and adversarial interactions in Ezra-Nehemiah, there is never a word of criticism toward the reigning monarch. This absence of condemnation points to the absolute power of the king. It would not have done at all to bite the hand that sustained one, even if that hand had turned against the whole endeavor. Such an absence may also point to a tension. It is in a sense in the shadow of the city of Babylon and by the grace of Babylon that the city of God, the "house of God," is reconstructed. It remains to be seen whether the vision of hope of a community coming into being as God's community could be maintained under this umbrella.

The areas of the land outside Jerusalem deserve special mention, since these play a certain role in the story described here. The northern part of the two kingdoms that existed in Israel had been devastated almost 150 years before the conquest of Jerusalem took place. The invading power of 722 had been Assyria. At that time many of the original inhabitants had been deported, others had remained in their place, and new inhabitants were imported. A mix of ethnic groups ensued, which caused some of the hostility expressed in Ezra-Nehemiah between those from outside Jerusalem, sometimes located in Samaria, sometimes called "the people of the land," and the group that was working to restore temple, city, and community. The hostility originated now in one group, then in another, according to the accounts. In Ezra 4 groups of these people approach the "returned exiles" and are rebuffed. In Nehemiah 2, 4, and 6 the animosity originated in Samaria, specifically with the governor of that province, Sanballat. At stake here are relations with immediate neighbors. But above all, these relations raised the issue of identity for the community of the returned exiles, if not in a new way, then certainly with new emphasis and new restrictions. Identity in Ezra-Nehemiah is a question of who is inside and who belongs outside; hence also the long lists of names, hence also the term "holy seed," which stands in contrast to "the peoples of the lands." Separation has become an important concept.

THE PEOPLE

Ezra and Nehemiah present a bewildering array of names. Many of them occur in long lists. It will help to sort these names into different groups and characters. There are three main groups: the returning exiles and their eventual descendants; the groups in the surrounding areas, including Samaria, which might include descendants of the original population, imported folk, and a mix of these two categories; last, there is the entourage of the Persian monarch, representing his interest and his power.

The Returning Exiles

These folk have leaders who are listed by name (Ezra 1:8 and 2:2 and Neh. 7:7) and ancestral lineage that is introduced by name (Ezra:2:3ff. and Neh. 7:8ff.). Being recorded as belonging to this lineage was extremely important, and not being found in the genealogical records might mean exclusion from the group (See Ezra 2:59–63). The leaders may also be indicated by the general name "leaders," "heads of families," "elders," or "officials." The settlers of Jerusalem and Judah were classified according to functions, the most important among them being the priesthood. Next came the Levites, who served under the priests. The priests began the task of organized worship even before the temple reconstruction was started (Ezra 3:2ff.) and via the Levites oversaw the work of rebuilding. In Nehemiah 3, the priests themselves are said to rebuild. Whether they actually did so or rather were in charge of the project while others in fact did the work we do not know, but the phrasing is significant. Builders are named elaborately in Nehemiah 3, which highlights the importance of this task and the people involved in it. Certain groupings are represented by the number twelve, symbolic for all Israel (Ezra 2:1; 6:17; Neh. 7:7).

Different classes of folk are mentioned, such as "temple singers," "temple servants," "gatekeepers," to indicate the totality of the classes included in the return. A striking variety of terms is used to indicate the community as a totality: "the people," (Ezra 3:1; Neh. 8:1–12, for example); or "all the people" (Ezra 3:11; 9:9; Neh. 8:1–12, for example); or "the people of Israel" (Ezra 2:2; 6:16, 21; 9:1, for example); or "the returned exiles" (Ezra 4:1; 8:35; 10:16, for example); or "the assembly" (Neh. 7:66) to indicate the community as a totality. These are also called "the Jews" (Ezra 4:12, 23; 6:14; Neh. 2:16; 4:1; 6:6; 13:23), the word in Hebrew being Judahites, that is, those from Judah. It is only during and after this period that the designation "Jews" for the ancient covenant community of Israel becomes appropriate. There is a strong emphasis on the community, its participation in all the endeavors, the building, the festivals, the repairs, the social and religious reforms, throughout Ezra and Nehemiah. In Ezra 2:64 and Nehemiah 7:66 the entire community is counted at 49,697. Scholars have estimated that the population of Judah could have been approximately 20,000 at the beginning of this period and around 50,000 in the fourth century B.C.E. This difference could be reflected in Ezra 2, where the number totals 29,818 if one counts the names mentioned in verses 2–58, but 49,697 when recorded in verse 64. Or the higher number could include women, for they are not recorded in the lists by name.

Women are present in these texts only when they are specifically mentioned, as in Ezra 2:65; 10:1, and Nehemiah 3:12; 5:1; 7:67, for example. In Ezra 9 and 10 women are present as a group of "foreign women." In Ezra 10 it is especially noteworthy that the males who had married "foreign women" are mentioned by name, but not the women who were sent into exile (Ezra 9:18–43). The only woman mentioned by name in Ezra-Nehemiah is a prophet named by Nehemiah as one of his antagonists (Neh. 6:14). The impression is one of overwhelming male presence and male significance.

The Inhabitants
of the Neighboring Areas

This group, both in the south and the north, including Samaria, generally receives negative mention. It is not at all clear where those who had originally remained behind in Judah fit in. Deportations like those imposed during the Babylonian conquest in the first decades of the sixth century were never total. A community of people would be left behind, especially in the rural areas. There is a mention in Nehemiah 1:3 of "the survivors," a category that may include descendants of those who had originally returned from exile and of those who had never been in captivity. Nowhere else is there mention of inhabitants who receive the returning exiles or who are greeted by them with encouragement and approval. Generally, the groups in the surrounding areas are depicted in Ezra-Nehemiah as hostile. They are indicated by the term "the neighboring peoples" (Ezra 3:3) or "the people of the land" (Ezra 4:4) and are introduced in Ezra 4 with the straightforward term "the adversaries of Judah and Benjamin." It is an important matter for the community in Judah to "separate itself" from these groups (Ezra 6:21; 9:1ff.). According to the text, it is because of interference from individuals among these circles that the first attempts at restoring the temple are halted (Ezra 4). Nehemiah especially suffers personally from plots of individuals who range themselves against him and the community (Neh. 2:10; 4:1ff.; 6:1–14). The implications in Nehemiah are that personal jealousy was involved.

It is not entirely clear in these reports how much of the hostility was one-sided and how much of it arose from the zeal for identity and belonging that caused the community in Judah to look inward rather than outward.

Persian Imperial Power

This forms the third significant group in Ezra-Nehemiah. By all logic this group should have solicited the most severe criticism, the deepest hostility. Even if Persia was not identical to the original conqueror of Jerusalem, Babylon, still it was the overlord, the foreign occupying power that literally had Judah and Jerusalem in its possession. Yet no hostility toward Persia is evident from the biblical text. This absence of strong resistance to Persia and its rulers may be due partly to the liberality of the monarchs, beginning with Cyrus (Ezra 1), and their provisions for a return of the exiles and a rebuilding of temple and city. But in addition, the powerlessness of the community in Judah in terms of rebellion against the overwhelming reality of Persian domination must have played a role. Quarreling with Persia could result in certain, final destruction and an end to all hopes and dreams of rebuilding a community on the ruins of the old. When quarrels broke out, they were rather with immediate neighbors through whom the reigning powers could be manipulated for or against the efforts of the Jews. Practically speaking, the restoration of any community in Judah/Jerusalem could take place only in the shadow of Babylon.

Governors were the administrative overseers of a given province of the kingdom. These governors were responsible to someone called a satrap who was directly responsible to the king. Governors of Judah may have been Jews or not, according to who seemed the most judicious appointment. Governors, then, signal Persian presence in the text of Ezra-Nehemiah, albeit not always as a member of this group. Most of the time Persian presence is signaled in these books via individuals rather than groups. A few times the text mentions "soldiers and cavalry" (Ezra 8:22 and Neh. 1:9), but mostly Persia is represented by those individuals who embody its power, the monarchs. Second, the Persian overlord is visible in the story through his appointees.

The cast of characters, then, includes at least four and perhaps five kings: Cyrus (550–530); Darius (522–486); Ahasuerus = Xerxes (486–465); Artaxerxes (465–424); and possibly Artaxerxes II (404–358). The kings are presented through the letters they write, all of which are decrees. Through their documents it appears that Cyrus was by far the most generous and benevolent. One of the Artaxerxes characters was the most fearful and presented therefore the greatest hindrance to the restoration projects. Darius proved himself to be open to persuasion in favor of the Jews, especially when the authority of his predecessor, Cyrus, was brought into play (Ezra 6). A second Artaxerxes seems generous and kind (Nehemiah 2), almost naive. Between them, these rulers span a range of dispositions and inclinations, depending on who advises them, or possibly on the extent to which they feel they can afford to be generous in terms of prudent government of a large empire. Although it is difficult to ascertain the accuracy of the reported generosity of the kings, it is certain that without the active support of the Persian government, the restoration in Judah could not have happened.

Other characters that must be ranged on the side of the foreign powers are the trouble makers described in Ezra: Rehum and Shimshai with their "associates" (Ezra 4:7–24). More neutral and therefore helpful are Tattenai and Shethar-bozenai and their "associates" who urge king Darius to search the royal archives for such authority as Cyrus may have given for the rebuilding (Ezra 5:3–17). In Nehemiah, Sanballat, the governor of Samaria, and his friend Tobiah, another official, are a constant source of hostility and treachery for Nehemiah; they are especially effective because they are related by family to members of the Judahite community (Neh. 2:10; 4:1–23; 6:1–14; 13:4–9).

Leadership

The most important leaders of the returned exiles were Ezra and Nehemiah themselves. Of the two, Ezra is named a priest and a scribe (Ezra 7:6, 11; Neh. 8:1, 2), thus incorporating in himself the most important functions for the period of the restoration of Judah/Jerusalem. His lineage is carefully recorded as going back to Aaron, the traditional founder of the priestly house (Ezra 7:1), and his expertise regarding the Torah is mentioned several times (Ezra 7:10, 25). In the book of Nehemiah, Ezra appears accompanied by a representative group of laymen and Levites at the public recital of the Torah (Neh. 8:4, 7). Ezra appears usually surrounded by members of his group. Although he was clearly an individual and is present as such in the text, especially in the first person account (Ezra 7:27–9:15), the distinction between him and his community is not always sharply drawn. The interest of the reader is drawn more to the importance and activity of the community than to those of the leaders.

Nehemiah was a Jew who had risen to a high position at the Persian court and who was appointed eventually as governor over Judah. This appointment may have put him in a somewhat strained position, because he would have to keep loyalty both with the foreign power and with his community in Judah. The first person account of Nehemiah is longer than that of Ezra and stretches from Nehemiah 1—7, to be interrupted and continued again in 11:1 until the end of the book. Nehemiah is more present as an individual than Ezra in the material but at times strikes one as somewhat self-serving with his frequent pleas for vengeance on others and protection for himself (Neh. 4:4, 5; 5:19; 6:14; 13:14).

AUTHORSHIP

In terms of the questions raised at the outset, we know some things about Ezra and Nehemiah. They were Jews who chose to return to Judah when they saw the opportunity and when they had the support of the reigning power. There they oversaw and guided the restoration of important structures and reforms of the community. Their lifetime we can put in a period somewhere between 500 and 400 B.C.E. without being able to fix the dates more precisely. A further question we might ask is whether Ezra and Nehemiah were involved in the writing of the books named after them. Unfortunately, we do not know who was the author of Ezra-Nehemiah, nor when the writing was accomplished. There are those who believe that the same hand composed the books of Chronicles as well as Ezra and Nehemiah, and there are those who just as firmly believe that this is not true.

The content of Ezra-Nehemiah provides letters, lists of families and individuals, as well as accounts of events in the third person and accounts in the first person. A number of the letters are written in the Aramaic rather than Hebrew language (Ezra 4:7–6:18). I suggest that a writer or editor combined the different materials, perhaps on the basis of the so-called Ezra and Nehemiah memoirs, which may well have been original to Ezra and Nehemiah themselves, weaving them together with existing official documents, genealogical lists, and third person accounts into the books of Ezra and Nehemiah as we now know them. This editing and writing process may have taken place in the early part of the fourth century B.C.E.

THEOLOGY

God is first of all presented in this material as the divine initiator. It is through God's inspiration that events are set in motion. God is said to have stirred up the spirit of Cyrus before he issues his decree for the first return (Ezra 1:1; see also Ezra 6:22). Subsequently, God inspired the exiles to return to Jerusalem (Ezra 1:5). Divine initiative combining with human cooperation to achieve certain goals is a familiar theme in the Bible. A newer note is struck in Ezra-Nehemiah in that God's will for the community is deduced from the written word. A perspective prevails in Ezra-Nehemiah that viewed the destruction of the past as a deserved punishment from God's hand because of disobedience on the part of the people. It is a view that one can find in the Bible, especially in the book of Deuteronomy. It was understood then in the restoration community to be of the utmost importance not to repeat the mistakes of the past, but to follow faithfully the regulations laid down for the people in the directives God gave them through Moses, especially in terms of proper worship, the most obviously neglected aspect of life in exile. These regulations, the "statutes and ordinances" (Ezra 7:10), are followed on the authority of the document called the "book of the law of Moses" (Neh. 8:1). We will explore carefully the importance and implications of the central place of this document in Ezra-Nehemiah. God is seen in these books especially as the Deity who had long ago provided directives for the life of the community through God's servant Moses. These directives, interpreted and applied to the new context, will provide the restored community with dependable guidelines for its life together and for its life with God. Whether the experiment of the restoration will succeed will depend on following these guidelines.

We turn now to the text of Ezra and Nehemiah to fill in with more detail what I have outlined here.

1. A House in Jerusalem
Ezra 1—6

The first six chapters of Ezra concern themselves with the restoration of the temple in Jerusalem by a group of returned exiles from Babylon. This return, the first to occur in this material, is made possible by King Cyrus of Persia and takes place under his reign in 539 B.C.E. The exiles are not only allowed to return to Judah and Jerusalem but are under a charge by the king to rebuild the "house of God" and are given liberal provisions to make the rebuilding possible. The restoration runs into difficulties and is halted for a period of time. Eventually, under the reign of King Darius, the project is brought to completion in 515 B.C.E.

GOING HOME
Ezra 1

The Scene (1:1)

> 1:1 **In the first year of King Cyrus of Persia, in order that the word of the LORD by the mouth of Jeremiah might be accomplished, the LORD stirred up the spirit of King Cyrus of Persia so that he sent a herald throughout all his kingdom, and also in a written edict declared:**

Ezra 1 contains three distinct parts. The first sentence sets the scene, giving all the information necessary for the listener or reader to know the who, the when, the where, and even the why of what is to come. Then follows a written document, one of many in the Ezra-Nehemiah material (Ezra 1:2–4). The third part is made up of a description of the immediate effects of the document (1:5–11).

The opening verse of Ezra 1 is packed with information. Because of the terseness of the style, the reader is tempted to skip over the details; it is only when we unpack the sentence that we get a clearer picture. The first item provided is a date—the first year of King Cyrus, which puts the year in 539 B.C.E. The text places the events that will unfold clearly in time and also in space by naming Cyrus "king of Persia." Cyrus makes his proclamation because the Lord "stirred up" his spirit. This is one of the few times that God influences the action directly in Ezra or Nehemiah. Besides being called "the Lord," and "the God of Israel," God is indicated with the title "the God of heaven" in this chapter. This title indicates something larger than a God concerned only with a small group of people in a small corner of the earth. God, the God of heaven, who is also the God of Israel, is the one who arouses Cyrus to say what he says and do what he does—permitting the exiles to go home, to Jerusalem.

In addition, the opening announcement of Ezra puts the actions and words of Cyrus in agreement with a prophecy of Jeremiah. In Jeremiah 25:11 and 29:10 we find a duration predicted for the Exile and an announcement of a return. In addition, Isaiah 41:2, 25 and 45:13 use the exact phrasing in connection with Cyrus that occurs in Ezra 1:1: God is said there to "stir up," or "arouse," Cyrus. These connections with prophetic material are important because they put the events to come in a context of God's promises for the community. What happens here is understood by the writer of Ezra not just as a series of random events; neither are they purely secular events. Everything that happens here happens because of God's concern with God's people, a concern that stretches both into the past and the future.

The last part of the sentence describes a proclamation that issues from Cyrus throughout his entire realm, in oral as well as written form. Written directives make up one of the major themes of the Ezra-Nehemiah material. At the heart of these documents stands the one document that matters most to the returned exiles: the written directives from God to Moses—the law, or Torah. A number of other, lesser documents circle around the Torah, as planets around the sun, many of them letters from Persian royals that have the power to set activities in motion or stop them. The first of these letters is the proclamation of Cyrus, published in all his realm. You could say that of all the royal letters this one is the most important, for without it nothing that is described here would have happened.

What are some implications of this information? It may feel odd to us to date events by the year of a certain king's reign. In biblical times, however, this was the customary way to provide dates. The prophetic books in the Bible ordinarily open with a setting of the prophet's activity "in the days of . . . " one king or another (see Isa. 1:1; Jer. 1:1–3; Dan. 1:1; Hos. 1:1, for example). The dating found in those books referred the listener or reader to the reign of the kings in ancient Israel. After the Babylonian Exile, which began around 597 B.C.E., kingship disappeared from Israel. Henceforth, time references must be to a foreign ruler. The events of which the book of Ezra speaks take place under the headline of the reign of "King Cyrus of Persia." Four out of the five times that Cyrus is spoken of in Ezra 1, he is called "King Cyrus of Persia." This repetition is not accidental, nor is it intended to convey information so much as to underline the reality of the context for the survivors of the Exile, wherever they live. As it is expressed in Nehemiah: "Here we are, slaves to this day—slaves in the land that you gave to our ancestors to enjoy its fruit and its good gifts. Its rich yield goes to the kings whom you have set over us because of our sins; they have power also over our bodies and over our livestock at their pleasure, and we are in great distress" (Neh. 9:36–37). This stark reality is evident from Ezra 1 in a more indirect way by its repeated reference to Cyrus as king of Persia.

The Letter (1:2–4)

> 1:2 "Thus says King Cyrus of Persia: The LORD, the God of heaven, has given me all the kingdoms of the earth, and he has charged me to build him a house at Jerusalem in Judah. ³ Any of those among you who are of his people—may their God be with them!—are now permitted to go up to Jerusalem in Judah, and rebuild the house of the LORD, the God of Israel—he is the God who is in Jerusalem; ⁴ and let all survivors, in whatever place they reside, be assisted by the people of their place with silver and gold, with goods and with animals, besides freewill offerings for the house of God in Jerusalem."

Besides emphasizing the reality of Persian power, the text points also to God's power. This fact is evident not only from the opening lines but also from the letter that follows (Ezra 1:2–4). It is God who stirred the spirit of Cyrus, who has given Cyrus his vast realm (1:2). That is to say that Cyrus has power over his realm by God's grace. Stories in the Bible are told in such a way that one story easily connects to another. One story that dominates the biblical text and sets a pattern for other stories to follow is that of the exodus. Ezra 1 presents a picture of a new exodus with significant differences. The exodus from Egypt depicts a group's liberation by God's hand from a "house of bondage," to gain a new home in the land of God's promise. In this endeavor, the ruler of that day, Pharaoh of Egypt, provided the obstacle to release and freedom. Ezra 1, on the other hand, depicts a community that seeks to rebuild a destroyed home with the help of the ruler of that day, Cyrus. Where Pharaoh did everything he could to prevent the people from leaving, Cyrus does everything he can to make the people's departure easier, including provisions of financial assistance and restitution of lost possessions (Ezra 1:4, 6—11). The stories of deliverance are connected but not identical, and the patterns are repeated with variations. In both cases, the exodus from Egypt and the return from exile in Babylon, God is said to have influenced the ruler of the time, to contrasting effect.

In going home, the survivors of the Exile are going to a homeless place in a sense; the survivors have no houses, no homes, and neither does God. The first activity that Cyrus mentions in his letter is the building of a house for God. When the permission for the people to return is given, it is in order to rebuild the same house. The term "house" in connection with God signals another important repetition in the chapter. Five times in ten verses the house of God in Jerusalem is mentioned in some way. This house is among the most severe losses that the community sustained during the Babylonian conquest. At the time that I write these words, there has been a series of church burnings in the southern United States. To date, more than seventy churches, especially of African-American communities, have been destroyed by fire. As modern believers, we understand that God does not live in a church or in any particular place. The phrase "he is the God who is in Jerusalem" (Ezra 1:3) from Cyrus may strike us as naive. Nevertheless, the destruction of sanctuaries, especially if it appears deliberate, strikes at the heart of a community because it is an assault on what we hold as sacred and what binds us together as a community. Ancient Israelite believers too understood that God did not live in a temple. "Even heaven and the highest heaven cannot contain you, how much less this house that I have built!" King Solomon prayed according to the Chronicler (2 Chron. 6:18). On the other hand, the temple represented for ancient Israel the presence of what they held sacred. The temple had been an essential and visible symbol of God's presence. The first task then for the returned exiles was to rebuild the sanctuary, the house of God. Of course, there are some dangers in attaching too much importance to a building, even a sanctuary.

Besides its symbolic importance, the temple functioned also as the center of worship. We do not know exactly how and where the remnant of the community worshiped after the Babylonian conquest. For prayer and religious recital, a sanctuary or temple is not absolutely required. But it is certain that the worship as it had been organized and conducted at the preexilic temple had come to an end, at least temporarily. Before the Babylonian

Exile, worship had centered around sacrifice, both animal sacrifice and grain offering. With temple and altar gone, sacrificial worship could not be conducted. The loss of organized worship as they had known it was a profound one for the community, and it was of the utmost importance to restore the place where worship could be reorganized.

From Babylonia
to Jerusalem (1:5–11)

1:5 The heads of the families of Judah and Benjamin, and the priests and the Levites—everyone whose spirit God had stirred—got ready to go up and rebuild the house of the LORD in Jerusalem. 6 All their neighbors aided them with silver vessels, with gold, with goods, with animals, and with valuable gifts, besides all that was freely offered. 7 King Cyrus himself brought out the vessels of the house of the LORD that Nebuchadnezzar had carried away from Jerusalem and placed in the house of his gods. 8 King Cyrus of Persia had them released into the charge of Mithredath the treasurer, who counted them out to Sheshbazzar the prince of Judah. 9 And this was the inventory: gold basins, thirty; silver basins, one thousand; knives, twenty-nine; 10 gold bowls, thirty; other silver bowls, four hundred ten; other vessels, one thousand; 11 the total of the gold and silver vessels was five thousand four hundred. All these Sheshbazzar brought up, when the exiles were brought up from Babylonia to Jerusalem.

The third part of Ezra 1 tells of the activity of the people of Judah and Jerusalem and how the king equips them for their task (Ezra 1:5–11). Again, we are reminded of the difference between this king and the Pharaoh in the exodus story. Cyrus goes so far as to retrieve the booty that the Babylonian king had stolen for his own house of worship. Lists begin to occur for the first time. If one totals the number of items listed in verses 9 and 10, it comes to less than the number cited in verse 11; a first instance in Ezra of discrepancies in figures. Just as the writers of these texts were not interested first of all in exact chronology, so the lists may have been presented for other reasons than exact numbers. In Ezra 1:8–11 the text conveys the generosity of Cyrus of the new story, in contrast to Pharaoh of the old story, and the fact that the exiles did not return empty-handed. This too had been a feature of the old story (Exod. 3:22 and 12:35–36), but then the "gifts" from neighbors had been given under duress and were called "plunder." Now, gifts, old and new, are provided as free assistance to the returning exiles. The neighbors, people of their place, whether they were

Jews or Persians we do not know, aided them. In Hebrew the phrase for "aided them" is "strengthened their hands."

The people who prepare to return to Jerusalem are represented by "the heads of the families of Judah and Benjamin," the two tribes that would henceforth be representative of the original twelve tribes of Israel. Judah and Benjamin now will be "the people Israel." These household heads have their spirit stirred by God. As God stirred the spirit of Cyrus, so now God activates the returnees according to the text, thus again assigning an essential initiative to God. Verse 5 tellingly also mentions the priests and the Levites, those who are crucial for a resumption of worship in the old style and altogether a group that is central for the accounts of Ezra and Nehemiah. In the end all is ready for a well-prepared execution of the plans: the heads of the families, including priests and Levites, are ready to go; king Cyrus himself retrieves furnishings for the house that is to be built; king Cyrus releases them to a treasurer, who gives them to the expedition leader, Sheshbazzar; Sheshbazzar then guides the expedition.

It is not altogether clear who Sheshbazzar was or what he did, in spite of the fact that he is called a "prince of Judah" and in chapter 5 is mentioned again as "governor of Judah" and as one who laid the foundations of the temple (Ezra 5:14). There is contradictory evidence in the Bible that someone called Zerubbabel began the restoration (Ezra 3:2; 4:3; 5:2; also Hag. 1:14 and Zech. 4:9). Once more, we encounter confusing information. This time, it could be that the actual personalities of the leaders are not as important as we would think. Just as three Persian rulers are made to sound like one in Ezra 6:14, two leaders of the expedition from Babylon to Jerusalem are not clearly distinguished from one another. The participation of the leaders in this story is not as significant apparently as the participation of the community. Sheshbazzar disappears in the long family list that follows.

FAMILY BY FAMILY
Ezra 2

When I was growing up in The Netherlands, we kept the custom in our family of reading a section of Scripture aloud after the evening meal. Among my mother's relatives there reputedly had been a cousin who upon reaching a text with Hebrew names would solemnly intone "difficult word" and skip to the next section. We might well want to do the same with the second chapter of

Ezra. It all seems one long "difficult word." Who among us is eager to wade through this material? Can we just take it for granted that a lot of different folk from different families and towns returned to Judah and Jerusalem and settled there? The problem with skipping sections such as these is that we might just miss an important bit of information.

First, Ezra and Nehemiah like to list people and things; they tie matters together by reciting lists and tidying up untidy circumstances. Genealogical lists also witness to the fact that record keeping was of great importance in that time as a natural follow-up to the chaos of war and deportation. Second, it becomes increasingly important to prove that one belongs inside the circle. The notion of identity takes on a life of its own in this material, and one testimony to this idea consists of the genealogies. Third, lists are important in order to highlight certain functions; we note once more the mention of priests and Levites.

In addition, this particular list is also of interest because of whom it excludes. In a brief section toward the end, a group of people appears named with their towns, Babylonian towns this time. These folk have the misfortune of not being able to prove that they belong to Israel. They do not have the necessary papers! "They could not prove their families or their descent, whether they belonged to Israel" (2:59). Among them were descendants of priests. "These looked for their entries in the genealogical records, but they were not found there, and so they were excluded from the priesthood as unclean; the governor told them that they were not to partake of the most holy food, until there should be a priest to consult Urim and Thummim" (2:62–63). This episode strikes an ominous note. Here were those who were eager to belong. They did research, but either their records had never existed or they were destroyed. Or perhaps these folk were indeed of mixed descent. It is the first instance of exclusion in the Ezra-Nehemiah material for the sake of keeping the community separate. It will not be the last.

The chapter ends on a positive note, with the group of returnees donating liberally for the sake of the rebuilding of the "house of God." The entire community takes responsibility for the enterprise. The last verse conveys almost a sense of tranquillity: "The priests, the Levites, and some of the people lived in Jerusalem and its vicinity; and the singers, the gatekeepers, and the temple servants lived in their towns, and all Israel in their towns" (2:70). We note once more how groups are listed according to their function, especially those in some way connected with the apparatus of worship.

LAYING THE FOUNDATIONS
Ezra 3

Building the Altar: (3:1–7)

3:1 **When the seventh month came, and the Israelites were in the towns, the people gathered together in Jerusalem.** 2 **Then Jeshua son of Jozadak, with his fellow priests, and Zerubbabel son of Shealtiel with his kin set out to build the altar of the God of Israel, to offer burnt offerings on it, as prescribed in the law of Moses the man of God.** 3 **They set up the altar on its foundation, because they were in dread of the neighboring peoples, and they offered burnt offerings upon it to the LORD, morning and evening.**

The time marker in the first verse of this chapter indicates the seventh month. The seventh month, September/October (Hebrew: Tishri), marks one of the most significant times in terms of the liturgical year. The book of Numbers provides the regulations for this month, which include convocations, different types of sacrifices, the Day of Atonement, and the Feast of Booths (see Numbers 29). It is significant that precisely in this month the people "gathered together" (the Hebrew literally reads "as one man"). Once the convocation is in place, the lack of a worship center becomes glaringly obvious.

First things first, then. The decision is made to build at least an altar so worship can be carried out properly. The people gather together for the task, which takes place under the guidance of religious and political leadership: Jeshua, the priest, and Zerubbabel, the Jewish governor. From this short passage, it is apparent how important it was to establish the link with the tradition of the past. The worship of the past had been marked especially by sacrifice. For sacrifice, personnel and the appropriate apparatus are needed. That priests and Levites are available has been made abundantly clear in the account already. What is still lacking is the altar. When the old temple, constructed under king Solomon, was destroyed, it was burned according to the biblical record (2 Kings 25:9). There is no mention of "razing," a more thorough method of destroying a building. Since the temple and the altar were made of stone, much of their foundations and some of the outer structure may have been preserved. It was not difficult then to discern the site of the altar and begin constructing a new one. How much time the construction of the altar took is not clear and in part would depend on how much of the old structure had remained standing. Today, we may envision an altar as a sort of table in the front, inside the sanctuary. In biblical times, however, altars were separate stone structures, outside of the temple, themselves the size of a small building around which and on which all the officially prescribed activities of offerings took place. Formal, permanent altars, attached to a sanctuary, were large.

In this section of Ezra, one phrase in particular draws our attention. The writer states that they constructed the altar "because they were in dread of the neighboring peoples" (Ezra 3:3). This seems a strange motivation for the building of the altar. It is clear that there must have been a desire to reinstate the prescribed liturgical practices. How, then, would the neighbors affect these practices?

Because deportations of conquered peoples were never total, the neighboring peoples would consist of those left behind after the Babylonian conquest (See 2 Kings 25:12), of immigrants into the region, and of a mix of the two. Since the issue in this section of Ezra is worship practices, it must be that the practices of the neighboring peoples were suspect in the eyes of the returned exiles. They do not want to join the life of worship that is conducted among them, are afraid what idolatry this might lead them to, and want to reinstate the sacrificial cult according to "the law of Moses the man of God" (Ezra 3:2).

This is the first time that the law and Moses are mentioned in Ezra. The lines are being drawn sharply, as to who belongs in the circle of the family of the God of Israel, and as to what constitutes appropriate worship. The law of Moses, the Torah, will at every point be the touchstone for the life of the community and for the manner in which they conduct the worship. The continuity of the community in Judah with the past is guaranteed to a great degree by its adherence to the written law. Yet the law was not one thing. It too had evolved over hundreds of years and showed a variety of directives on certain issues, especially on how to live with "strangers."

But for now, things seem off to a good start, so that the rhythm of daily sacrifice and special festivals can be reestablished (Ezra 3:4–7). The first celebration is the festival of booths, a feast with agricultural roots that mainly celebrated the deliverance from captivity in Egypt. Small wonder that this is the first festival to be celebrated among the newly delivered captives who have returned to Jerusalem. The story of God with God's people has not come to an end and is continuing to unfold to the great rejoicing of the people.

Building the Temple (3:8–13)

3:8 In the second year after their arrival at the house of God at Jerusalem, in the second month, Zerubbabel son of Shealtiel and Jeshua son of Jozadak

made a beginning, together with the rest of their people, the priests and the Levites and all who had come to Jerusalem from the captivity. They appointed the Levites, from twenty years old and upward, to have the oversight of the work on the house of the LORD. ⁹And Jeshua with his sons and his kin, and Kadmiel and his sons, Binnui and Hodaviah, along with the sons of Henadad, the Levites, their sons and kin, together took charge of the workers in the house of God.

¹⁰ When the builders laid the foundation of the temple of the LORD, the priests in their vestments were stationed to praise the LORD with trumpets, and the Levites, the sons of Asaph, with cymbals, according to the directions of King David of Israel; ¹¹ and they sang responsively, praising and giving thanks to the LORD,

"For he is good,
    for his steadfast love endures forever toward Israel."

And all the people responded with a great shout when they praised the LORD, because the foundation of the house of the LORD was laid. ¹² But many of the priests and Levites and heads of families, old people who had seen the first house on its foundations, wept with a loud voice when they saw this house, though many shouted aloud for joy, ¹³ so that the people could not distinguish the sound of the joyful shout from the sound of the people's weeping, for the people shouted so loudly that the sound was heard far away.

Now the real work on the temple can begin, and so it does indeed, in the second year of the return. The work is started in the second month, April/May (Hebrew: Ziv), which was also the month that Solomon had begun to construct the temple (1 Kings 6:1; 2 Chron. 3:2). Continuity with the past is again established. The laying of the foundations itself is a cause of great joy. This work was perhaps more a matter of restoration than building from scratch, for the foundations would still have been there. (The preexilic temple was a huge structure; estimates are that it was 105 feet long, 52 feet high, and 30 feet wide.) This work will not be completed within a short period of time. They "made a beginning," the text records (Ezra 3:8).

The people that oversee the work are listed as Zerubbabel and Jeshua, the same figures who oversaw the building of the altar (3:8). Zerubbabel is the grandson of the exiled former king of Judah, and is at this time the appointed governor. Jeshua is the high priest. The two of them may themselves have participated in the work. Skilled workers would have been scarce, and it was probably necessary for all to pitch in and do their part, no matter what their rank. The community is involved in the work also, as the text notes: "together with the rest of their people, . . . and all who had come to Jerusalem from the captivity" (3:8).

The building of a new structure can be an exciting event. I remember as a small child how my parents had a new house built in a neighboring town and the solemn but joyful occasion on which my younger sister was granted the privilege to "lay the first stone." A small plaque was placed on that corner of the house to mark her name and the date. Perhaps we have seen pictures of barn raising in Amish communities, or witnessed them. Imagine how the community in Judah felt when they witnessed the laying of the first stone of the house of God! So there is weeping as the foundation is laid, as well as rejoicing. It is as if the house has already gone up, so that the writer can say "when they saw this house," even though only a beginning has been made (3:12). The text testifies to loud noise—music and singing and shouting. In fact, "the people shouted so loudly that the sound was heard far away" (Ezra 3:13).

THE WORK DISCONTINUED
Ezra 4

We Alone Will Build (4:1–5)

> 4:1 When the adversaries of Judah and Benjamin heard that the returned exiles were building a temple to the LORD, the God of Israel, 2 they approached Zerubbabel and the heads of families and said to them, "Let us build with you, for we worship your God as you do, and we have been sacrificing to him ever since the days of King Esar-haddon of Assyria who brought us here." 3 But Zerubbabel, Jeshua, and the rest of the heads of families in Israel said to them, "You shall have no part with us in building a house to our God; but we alone will build to the LORD, the God of Israel, as King Cyrus of Persia has commanded us."
>   4 Then the people of the land discouraged the people of Judah, and made them afraid to build, 5 and they bribed officials to frustrate their plan throughout the reign of King Cyrus of Persia and until the reign of King Darius of Persia.

A group comes and asks of the leadership in the community whether they may participate in the work. This request is turned down with sharp words. The Persian authorities are called in and the work stops. This is the story told in chapter 4. The account is not as straightforward as we may wish, so we need to do some disentangling of threads that are here woven together but may in fact originally belong to another story.

Naturally, a story is not interesting unless unforeseen difficulties arise that then have to be solved. So it is with this story. Ezra 4:1 introduces a group of people with the words "adversaries of Judah and Benjamin," without specifying further who these people are. Is this the same group as the one mentioned in 3:3, a group that had provided at least the partial motivation for the rebuilding of the altar? It is possible, especially because the group is called "the people of the land" in verse 4. Whatever their exact identity, their approach to the leaders of the community in Judah does not sound hostile. Then why are they called "adversaries"? Ostensibly, they want to join in the effort, for they want to worship the same God. King Esar-haddon was an Assyrian ruler in the first part of the seventh century B.C.E., and these folk claim they have worshiped the God of Israel since that time.

In 2 Kings 17:24–41 it is reported that peoples from other lands were imported into Samaria and the region around it, after the destruction of that city and the deportation of its inhabitants. These were instructed in the worship of the God of Israel and worshiped God but "also served their own gods, after the manner of the nations from among whom they had been carried away," according to 2 Kings 17:33. Is this the same group that approaches the builders of the temple in Jerusalem? Perhaps, and perhaps the reason for turning them down is the same as the reason for the earlier fear: The community in Jerusalem draws a tight line around its circle. The returned exiles are not interested in converts, in those who are outside the covenant community; rather, they are fearful of mixing with them. The good faith of the outsiders is not called into question in this account, but there is no flexibility on this issue among the returned exiles. In the end they will expel some from among their number, even some with the closest family ties, rather than risk contamination of themselves and their faith.

So the settlers do not mince words when they turn away the offer for help, an offer they could probably have used to great advantage: "You shall have no part with us. . . . we alone will build . . . " (Ezra 4:3). Naturally, this refusal creates resentment and hostility on the part of those who are turned away. Such treatment almost guarantees that the neighbors will henceforth have an adversarial attitude, even if they did not have one before. So they begin to frighten the builders—literally to "weaken their hands," in contrast to the neighbors in Persia who had "strengthened the hands" of the emigrants—and to intrigue with the Persian court.

We are not surprised at this hostile reaction. The attitude of the settlers in Judah strikes most of us probably as extreme and unnecessary, not easy to understand. We will meet the zeal for ethnic and religious purity in its most extreme form in the last chapters of Ezra and will consider the implications more closely when we reach that material.

At this point, it may help to be clear that Ezra-Nehemiah also reflect a historical situation. This situation grew over centuries in terms of a deepening rift between north and south in Israel and an eventual split between what became the Samaritan faction and the Jews in Judah and Jerusalem. The biblical account here explores some of the roots of this division. There were most likely hostile attitudes on both sides. In terms of an effort to reflect the beginnings of a split between two ethnic groups, this account is not a model so much as simply an attempt to relate how it happened.

Two Letters (4:6–24)

4:23 Then when the copy of King Artaxerxes' letter was read before Rehum and the scribe Shimshai and their associates, they hurried to the Jews in Jerusalem and by force and power made them cease. 24 At that time the work on the house of God in Jerusalem stopped and was discontinued until the second year of the reign of King Darius of Persia.

Most of chapter 4 consists of two letters that probably confuse many people. The plans of the builders are reportedly frustrated from the days of King Cyrus until Darius, that is, from 537 until 520, as we know from Ezra 4:24. In Ezra 4:6, without transition, a king by the name of Ahasuerus appears, and in verse 7 yet another ruler called Artaxerxes. If we check on dates, we have suddenly moved from 539 to 480, and again to 465 B.C.E. Where has king Cyrus gone? If we were reading in Hebrew, we would be even more confused, for in verse 8 the text shifts to the Aramaic language.

The two letters cited in Ezra 4:6–24 are prefaced by an allusion to another letter. Then follows the first missive from a group of schemers against the settlers in Judah. This letter accuses the returned exiles of rebuilding the city of Jerusalem with nefarious purposes. The second letter, from King Artaxerxes, agrees that nothing good will come of the effort to rebuild and gives permission to the writers of the accusation to issue an order for the work to be stopped. Note again how letters are important to the flow of the story. The problem for the reader is that the letters are clearly from different periods than the one the text has presented so far and, furthermore, that the issue of concern for the letter writers is not the building of a temple but the rebuilding of a city.

Recall that the writer of these accounts is not as much interested in chronology and that the overwhelming reality of the time was the Persian domination of Judah. A Persian ruler had given permission for the return and the rebuilding. By his authority the entire endeavor had been set in motion. A Persian ruler has also the power to stop the work. That is the reality reflected in Ezra 4:6–21. It does not take much effort for the "adversaries" to sow distrust in the mind of the overlord and have him issue a command to cease and desist.

Another reality that is reflected at this point in the story is that the work was indeed halted. How can we explain this? Was there originally a letter from King Cyrus to stop the endeavor, a letter that was lost in the archives? Were the neighbors more effective all by themselves, and is it too embarrassing to mention their success? Or was the group of settlers not effective enough, too small, too inexperienced? All of these are possible, and we must stay with the uncertainty of not really knowing what took place.

In terms of the subject of the two documents, we know that work on the city walls is described in Nehemiah rather than in Ezra. This work indeed took place during the reign of King Artaxerxes (465–424 B.C.E.), who also appointed Nehemiah as governor of Judah. The letters in Ezra 4 may well date from a period earlier in Artaxerxes' reign, roughly a century after Cyrus. The writer of Ezra felt apparently that they could be applied to the earlier situation and to problems with the restoration of the temple. The symbolic distinction between temple and city was most likely not sharply drawn. If the holiest location in the city was understood to be the temple, then by extension the entire city of Jerusalem was seen as holy and symbolic of God's presence. In Zechariah, a prophet of this period, we read for example: "Thus says the LORD: I will return to Zion, and will dwell in the midst of Jerusalem; Jerusalem shall be called the faithful city, and the mountain of the LORD of hosts shall be called the holy mountain" (Zech. 8:3).

As with the rebuilding of the altar and temple, we may discern practical as well as religious reasons for the restoration of the city. City walls served as a guarantee for the safety of the inhabitants. Walls kept unwanted folk out and the citizens inside safe, if all worked well. Repairing the city walls of Jerusalem in postexilic times was an obvious necessity. Because we think of city and temple in more practical terms, it may be difficult to understand the blurring of the distinction between the two. The holy aspect of the city and its walls becomes abundantly clear from the celebrations that accompany the completion of the restoration as mentioned in Nehemiah. The letters thus work well on a number of levels: They reflect the reality of Persian domination at all times (note the threefold mention of taxes in v. 13); they provide an explanation of the cessation of work on the temple indirectly; they point to the close connection of temple and city in their symbolic value.

THE HOUSE IS FINISHED
Ezra 5 and 6

A Search for Records (5:1—6:1–12)

Ezra 5 recounts resumption of the restoration of the temple and another exchange of letters. The time period is slightly after that of the first three chapters, the reign of King Darius (522–486 B.C.E.), successor to Cyrus, and the subject is once more the rebuilding of the temple. So we return to familiar territory. Zerubbabel and Shealtiel are again overseeing the work, and the enterprise is helped along by prophecies from Haggai and Zechariah. The builders proceed on a word from God before they have received permission from the Persian overlord. Interference, therefore, occurs, albeit of a neutral sort. A governor named Tattenai and his friends come to inquire who gave permission for the work; they subsequently write to King Darius to inquire whether such permission was indeed obtained from King Cyrus as the builders of the temple claim: "And now, if it seems good to the king, have a search made in the royal archives there in Babylon, to see whether a decree was issued by King Cyrus for the rebuilding of this house of God in Jerusalem. Let the king send us his pleasure in this matter" (Ezra 5:17).

The writers of the letter to King Artaxerxes in the previous chapter had also urged a search of the records, and that king found what he wanted, evidence that Jerusalem was a city not to be trusted. Or, at least, he said he found this evidence. King Darius has a search of the archives conducted, and the original decree is found and quoted here. We may assume that he too finds what he wanted and that the restoration of the Jerusalem temple seems to be in the interest of the empire. The version of Cyrus' decree cited here (6:3–5) expands somewhat on the earlier one by specifying the dimensions of the temple to be constructed. King Darius then affirms the decree of Cyrus and exceeds his predecessor in generosity by providing even more liberally for the building costs: "the cost is to be paid to these people, in full and without delay, from the royal revenue, the tribute of the province Beyond the River" (6:8). This welcome news for the settlers in Judah stands in sharp contrast to the decision by Artaxerxes not to delay in stopping the work. "Take care," that king cautioned, "not to be slack in this matter; why should damage grow to the hurt of the king?" (Ezra 4:22). From one extreme to another, the fickleness of those in power is demonstrated. In the meantime, we observe that Darius' generosity extended itself at Tattenai's cost, for it is his province that must provide the revenue. Not only is the building project to continue, but it is now well provided for.

The Task Accomplished (6:13–18)

6:13 **Then, according to the word sent by King Darius, Tattenai, the governor of the province Beyond the River, Shethar-bozenai, and their associates did with all diligence what King Darius had ordered.** [14] **So the elders of the Jews built and prospered, through the prophesying of the prophet Haggai and Zechariah son of Iddo. They finished their building by command of the God of Israel and by decree of Cyrus, Darius, and King Artaxerxes of Persia;** [15] **and this house was finished on the third day of the month of Adar, in the sixth year of the reign of King Darius.**

Now all comes together to create a successful completion. Tattenai and company do as they are bid by the king, the prophets Haggai and Zechariah do as they are bid by God, and the work continues. Divine inspiration and human authorization together create the possibility for success. The temple was finished on March 12, 515 B.C.E. Verse 14 recapitulates the important matters that have taken place. The ones in charge are the God of Israel and the Persian ruler. God provided the motivation, or, as is stated here, "the command." The decree is issued by power of the Persian overlord. Cyrus, Darius, and Artaxerxes are named as one, even though Artaxerxes' main contribution is yet to be recounted and he has so far had only a negative influence. (The reasons for conflating the three rulers are discussed in the introduction.) Also, the naming of Artaxerxes points to the future; there is yet work to be done. The holy place is not yet a home, without the restoration of the city. Yet, so far so good: "They finished their building . . . and this house was finished" (Ezra 6:14).

Now is the time for a celebration (Ezra 6:16–18). The first celebration is a ceremony of sacrifices (6:17). Then the priests and Levites are appointed to their appropriate tasks, "as it is written in the book of Moses" (6:18). In Exodus 29, Leviticus 8, Numbers 3, 4, and 8, provisions are cited for the division of the worship personnel into two classes: priests and Levites. Precise arrangements for their work were ordered by King David according to the biblical record (1 Chronicles 23–26). It is important, however, for the writer to refer to Moses and the Torah. Of all the decrees that occur in Ezra-Nehemiah, the Torah is the most significant. Also, by implication the reference to Moses draws the attention once

more to God, who is understood to be the author of the law. God's inspiration and direction thus surround all human activity in these verses.

The Lord Made Them Joyful (6:19–22)

6:19 **On the fourteenth day of the first month the returned exiles kept the
passover. ²⁰ For both the priests and the Levites had purified themselves; all
of them were clean. So they killed the passover lamb for all the returned exiles, for their fellow priests, and for themselves. ²¹ It was eaten by the people of Israel who had returned from exile, and also by all who had joined
them and separated themselves from the pollutions of the nations of the land
to worship the LORD, the God of Israel. ²² With joy they celebrated the festival of unleavened bread seven days; for the LORD had made them joyful,
and had turned the heart of the king of Assyria to them, so that he aided them
in the work on the house of God, the God of Israel.**

The next celebration is the all important one of Passover and marks the
first time that this festival is mentioned. For ancient Israel, Passover was
the festival that celebrated the deliverance from Egypt by God's hand and
the exodus (Exod. 12:1—13:16). It would have been for the community in
Judah *the* feast that celebrated deliverance from bondage and freedom
from oppression. The people are therefore named "the returned exiles" in
verse 19. At Passover, God's gracious activity in the past is gratefully remembered to lend hope for the future. This festival fits the occasion of the
finishing of God's house. Greater openness to others and readiness to
break the chain that fearfully excludes those who do not belong are shown
by the fact that for once the community embraces others and is not just
drawing its own circle tight (v. 21). It is God who has given them the joy
of this moment by motivating the spirit of the Persian ruler, here called
"the king of Assyria" (v. 22), not by mistake but in an attempt to stretch
the notion of foreign domination far back into the past, as well as to em-
brace the harm done to the neighbors in the north. The past is redeemed;
the future opens itself up to new possibilities.

2. Scribe of the Law of God
Ezra 7—10

If the first six chapters concern themselves with the reconstruction of the temple, Ezra 7—10 are about the reconstruction of the community in Jerusalem under the guidance of Ezra, the priest and "scribe of the law of God." A second return takes place following the one in the days of King Cyrus, this time under King Artaxerxes, whom we may assume to be the king who reigned from 465–424 and whom we met in a previous chapter (4:7–23). It is possible that the reference is to a later ruler, Artaxerxes II, who was in charge from 404–358 B.C.E., and that Ezra's mission and the return mentioned here took place more than fifty years later. Although we keep the possibility open, we use the earlier dating for the sake of a smooth description. However, the later dating is also a possibility.

Like the first return, the second one is set in motion by a letter from the king. As was noted in the second chapter, a list of families who accompany Ezra to Jerusalem punctuates the account of the journey home. Finally, issues of identity and purity arise with renewed force. These issues form the complication that needs to be resolved in this part of the story. The Torah as a guiding document comes to the fore in these chapters through the function of Ezra, who is its teacher and interpreter.

THE MISSION OF EZRA
Ezra 7:1–26

Ezra, Priest and Scribe (7:1–10)

> 7:1 After this, in the reign of King Artaxerxes of Persia, Ezra son of Seraiah, son of . . . 5 . . . son of the chief priest Aaron— 6 this Ezra went up from Babylonia. He was a scribe skilled in the law of Moses that the LORD the God of Israel had given; and the king granted him all that he asked, for the hand of the LORD his God was upon him.

[7] Some of the people of Israel, and some of the priests and Levites, the singers and gatekeepers, and the temple servants also went up to Jerusalem, in the seventh year of King Artaxerxes. [8] They came to Jerusalem in the fifth month, which was in the seventh year of the king. [9] On the first day of the first month the journey up from Babylon was begun, and on the first day of the fifth month he came to Jerusalem, for the gracious hand of his God was upon him. [10] For Ezra had set his heart to study the law of the LORD, and to do it, and to teach the statutes and ordinances in Israel.

These first ten verses describe Ezra, his lineage and present tasks, and his journey to Jerusalem with a group of companions, under the aegis of King Artaxerxes. The section anticipates what follows by announcing the arrival in Jerusalem (vv. 8–9), while the subsequent sections provide both the royal authorization for the journey (7:11–27) and details of the journey itself as well as the arrival (chap. 8).

It is clear that we cannot be sure of the exact time period for Ezra. The text names Artaxerxes as ruler, but since at least two kings by that name would be eligible, this naming only creates more uncertainty. Nevertheless, it is evident that the text has moved into a different time, a later one than the time of Cyrus, who authorized the first group of exiles to go back to Jerusalem. The opening verse indicates this change from one period to another with the vague "After this . . . " This is the second return of exiles from Judah mentioned in the Ezra-Nehemiah material. Not everyone was eager or ready at the first opportunity, in the days of Cyrus. Perhaps some folk had settled in Persia and were prospering. Moreover, another generation had grown up who had not themselves experienced the loss of their homeland. A long journey such as the one from Persia to Judah brought with it its own dangers and uncertainties. All these factors would weigh in when an opportunity for return presented itself. Not everyone left Persia, and the ones who left did not do so all at once.

The leader of the expedition this time is Ezra; Sheshbazzar had led the group of returning exiles under Cyrus. Six verses are spent on describing Ezra, and so we have a great deal of information about him, even if there is no pinpointing the dates of his activity. First, the text lists his ancestry, which has the effect of establishing Ezra firmly in the circle of the community of Israel. There is no doubt about his bloodlines. More important yet, his ancestry traces back to Aaron, and this establishes Ezra solidly in the priestly line. Priesthood was hereditary in ancient Israel, and Ezra has a full right to this inheritance. In the letter from Artaxerxes he is called "priest Ezra" (Ezra 7:11). Besides having this office, an office that had risen in importance in the community in Judah after the Babylonian Exile, Ezra is also called "a scribe." What sort of profession is that?

We, in the Christian community, may know scribes for the most part through the negative perspective from which they are viewed in the New Testament. There they are presented as opponents of Jesus and are described as frequently denounced by him. We may remember them from the list of "woes" in the Gospel of Matthew, for example, where the text repeats, "Woe to you, scribes and Pharisees, hypocrites!" (Matt. 23:13–36). In reality, a scribe was an important functionary in ancient societies. Scribes were persons who could read and write, but who also had competence in the areas they wrote about, as for example the law.

Scribes were attached to governments to keep the written records and engage in administration. A scribe was often also a scholar. In modern terms, a scribe was a combination of a secretary, a scholar, and a political figure. All these functions we must ascribe to Ezra when the writer calls him "a scribe." The identification does not stop there, however, but continues to define the subject of Ezra's skill: "the law of Moses" (Ezra 7:6). Whatever the exact time of Ezra's activities, it is certain that some form of the first five books of the Bible, not yet called the Bible at that time, existed in a written collection. This collection, from Genesis to Deuteronomy, was in its totality called the "law," or "instruction"; in Hebrew, "torah." The translation "law" is correct only in part, since these books contain a great deal of material other than law. This collection is the subject of Ezra's interest; he is both the person who copies the texts and the one who interprets and applies them, for he is "skilled in the law of Moses." The Torah came from Moses, according to the belief of the time, but the authority for it resided in God.

God is mentioned twice in verse 6, both times as the source of authority behind the human agent. The first time is in connection with the law of Moses, the second time with Ezra and the authority of the king. The king gave Ezra anything he asked for because "the hand of the LORD his God was upon him" (v. 7). In other words, God is the reason for the gracious behavior of the king. Ezra succeeded with his journey home for the same reason (v.9). "The hand of God" is a symbol for God's powerful and gracious presence. All the references to God indicate God as the ultimate authority and power behind and above all human agency.

The people are mentioned according to their groups and functions. People, priests and Levites, singers, gatekeepers and temple servants, all went up with Ezra on a journey that took approximately four to five months, the route being about nine hundred miles. Although Ezra is the leader, the distinction between himself and the community that returns is sometimes blurred. A plural verb in verse 8, "they came," changes to a singular verb, "he came," in verse 9. Ezra's significance lies not so much in being a leader of the expedition but in his skill with the Torah and his intention to teach it. It is his scribal function that is emphasized more than his priestly role. One gets the impression that Ezra was a priest by birth and a scribe by choice. He "had set his heart" according to the text, "to study," "to do," and "to teach" (v. 10). With this emphatic mention of Ezra's function and chosen task, the text implies that the community in Judah and Jerusalem were in need of a teacher of the Torah. This impression will find verification in the instruction Ezra receives from the king.

Instructions
from a King (7:11–26)

7:25 "And you, Ezra, according to the God-given wisdom you possess, appoint magistrates and judges who may judge all the people in the province Beyond the River who know the laws of your God; and you shall teach those who do not know them. 26 All who will not obey the law of your God and the law of the king, let judgment be strictly executed on them, whether for death or for banishment or for confiscation of their goods or for imprisonment."

Preceding these lines is a series of instructions from King Artaxerxes. To begin, the letter makes clear that Ezra, who is twice identified by all his functions (Ezra 7:11 and 12), is indeed sent by the king (7:14). Next, the letter spells out two tasks, one having to do with the Torah and one with the distribution of the gifts for the temple (7:14–20). Ezra is "to make inquiries about Judah and Jerusalem according to the law of your God, which is in your hand" (7:14). In so many words Ezra is charged to see whether the people are indeed living up to the demands that God makes of them. From the last lines of the letter, it becomes evident that this charge lies at the heart of his task. Ezra is to teach the laws and to check on the measure of obedience on the part of the Jewish community. He also receives authority to punish appropriately. Coming well supplied with gifts for the temple as he does, Ezra should have little difficulty receiving the respect from the community in Judah. The gifts thus have a double function: They not only supply the temple but they buttress Ezra's authority and serve to remove any potential distrust toward him from the Jerusalem community.

The middle section of the letter is devoted to instructions to the treasurers in that part of the realm to provide liberally for the temple and to refrain from taxing temple personnel (7:21–24). The provisions granted are again more liberal than those recorded in the decree of Darius (chap. 6), and we may probably take the amounts with a grain of salt. Yet the intention of the document at this point is plain. The royal master is inclined to generosity for the temple, as a kind of safeguard. It might not hurt to placate the people and the gods of the people in the realm, for who knows what vengeful forces may be unleashed otherwise (v. 23).

In this letter God is called "the God of heaven" or "your God" most frequently (vv. 12, 21, 23; 14, 17, 18, 25, 26), but also "the God of Israel" (v. 15); and there is a close connection between this God and Jerusalem, at least once God is identified as "the God of Jerusalem" (v. 19). There is reverence and respect here, but also a distancing on the part of the king as well as an inability to settle on one particular description. The letter does not identify this God as "the Lord," in Hebrew *Adonai*, as Cyrus' letter had done. This king deals with many different ethnic groups and their gods. It is best for the stability of the realm to provide for a way of life that is appropriate to their culture and religion. Ezra seems just the man to help with some settling down of what may be restless and rebellious elements.

THE JOURNEY HOME
Ezra 7:27—8:35

Ezra's Diary (7:27–28)

7:27 **Blessed be the LORD, the God of our ancestors, who put such a thing as this into the heart of the king to glorify the house of the LORD in Jerusalem,** [28] **and who extended to me steadfast love before the king and his counselors, and before all the king's mighty officers. I took courage, for the hand of the LORD my God was upon me, and I gathered leaders from Israel to go up with me.**

The text now switches to the first person singular and remains more or less in this mode through chapter 9 of the book. Scholars think that the source for these accounts was an actual journal or "memoir" written by Ezra himself. The writer of Ezra-Nehemiah wove material from such a journal together with a genealogical list (8:1–14) and a final third person account (chap. 10) to tell this story of the reconstruction of the community in Jerusalem.

In contrast to the way in which God is named in the letter of the king, the words of Ezra refer emphatically to God as "the LORD." Three times in two verses God is so named. For Ezra, God is not just the God of heaven or the God of Israel, but "the LORD, the God of our ancestors," the God who goes far back into the past of the community. The temple is "the house of the LORD," and finally he names God as "the LORD my God." The God of the community of the past who is worshiped in Jerusalem is also the personal God of Ezra, who is graciously and powerfully present with him. Out of that presence, that steadfast devotion, Ezra finds the courage to set out on the actual journey. Royal authority definitely takes a backseat to God's authority in this framework. We are constantly reminded that the subject of concern has changed from reconstructing an edifice to reshaping the community. To build "the house of God," both authority and funds from the ruling power were crucial; to build the community that worships in this house, different resources are necessary. It becomes essential to emphasize the way of life that identifies this community as the people Israel, the people who live in covenant with God. For this effort, the royal authorization and funds are largely irrelevant. "The law of God" will authorize their way of life and how they relate to one another, to their neighbors, and also to the foreign overlord. The question is: How can they shape and maintain an independent religious identity while politically and economically in a dependent state? This question is not unrelated to our contemporary situation, even though the contexts are vastly different. Today as well, religious communities wrestle with how to achieve or maintain a sense of their identity, in view of the pressure of the larger context. Churches in the late twentieth century, for example, struggle to take a clear position on issues such as divorce, sexual identity, or abortion, as a community with a Christian identity in distinction from the secular culture.

Once More the Families (8:1–20)

One way to preserve identity for the Jewish community in exile, for the exiles returning to Judah, is to look to their ancestral lines and to list the names of families who belong. So at this point, as earlier in the book, a list of family names follows. There are twelve families or clans named, representing the twelve tribes of Israel. Priests come first in this list (Ezra 8:1–14). When Ezra discovers there are no Levites, a special delegation procures the presence of this essential category of temple personnel (8:15–20). It seems as if Ezra is intent on observing an appropriate symbolic presence of Israel.

A Gathering at the River (8:21–36)

8:21 Then I proclaimed a fast there, at the river Ahava, that we might deny ourselves before our God, to seek from him a safe journey for ourselves, our children, and all our possessions. 22 For I was ashamed to ask the king for a

band of soldiers and cavalry to protect us against the enemy on our way, since we had told the king that the hand of our God is gracious to all who seek him, but his power and his wrath are against all who forsake him. [23] **So we fasted and petitioned our God for this, and he listened to our entreaty.**

Ezra's orientation is toward God rather than to secular authority. Before leaving the encampment at the river Ahava, he proclaims a fast. It is God, rather than the king, to whom Ezra and his companions turn for protection. Also, their safekeeping will be a kind of proof in the eyes of the Persians that God is indeed on Ezra's side. God is called "our God" at every turn in this passage. Fasting is perhaps not a custom very familiar to us. In ancient Israel fasting could accompany a variety of religious acts, such as mourning, penitence, or purification. Certain actions would accompany a fast, expressed with the words "to deny oneself" (Ezra 8:21; the Hebrew literally has "to afflict the self"), such as not eating or drinking, washing, anointing, wearing of sandals, and engaging in marital intercourse. The general goal of any fast was the same—to draw near to God and to draw God's attention. Fasting is naturally accompanied by prayer, therefore. The section thus ends by adding the mention of prayer: "we fasted and petitioned . . . " (8:23). The fast has been for the specific purpose of asking God's protection, since Ezra has boasted of this to the Persian power and was embarrassed, in light of his claim, to ask for secular protection.

Two further sections deal with the apportioning of the gifts to the appropriate people, the priests and the Levites who will actually bring them to Jerusalem, and with the arrival of the group that accompanies Ezra in the city: "Then we left the river Ahava on the twelfth day of the first month, to go to Jerusalem; the hand of our God was upon us, and he delivered us from the hand of the enemy and from ambushes along the way" (8:31). A sentence such as this one gives evidence of the dangers of the journey. Because God's protective presence is with them, the returnees reach Jerusalem safely and bring appropriate sacrifice. The time has come for Ezra to execute his proper task as teacher of the Torah.

THE LETTER OF THE LAW
Ezra 9 and 10

An Accusation Is Made (9:1–4)

9:1 **After these things had been done, the officials approached me and said, "The people of Israel, the priests, and the Levites have not separated themselves from the peoples of the lands with their abominations, from the**

Canaanites, the Hittites, the Perizzites, the Jebusites, the Ammonites, the Moabites, the Egyptians, and the Amorites. [2] For they have taken some of their daughters as wives for themselves and for their sons. Thus the holy seed has mixed itself with the peoples of the lands, and in this faithlessness the officials and leaders have led the way." [3] When I heard this, I tore my garment and my mantle, and pulled hair from my head and beard, and sat appalled. [4] Then all who trembled at the words of the God of Israel, because of the faithlessness of the returned exiles, gathered around me while I sat appalled until the evening sacrifice.

Up to this point, the text has presented a kind of prelude to the story that now develops. Complications arise that form barriers to the reconstruction of the community in Jerusalem, and the rest of the book of Ezra deals with these problems. The section begins with another time indicator, "After these things had been done" (9:1), ostensibly referring to the sacrificing mentioned immediately before. Many readers and interpreters of these texts believe, however, that the phrase refers to the reading of the law described in Nehemiah 8 and 9, because the account that follows would fit better after such an event. Yet there is nothing to prevent us from understanding the order of things as we read it here: Ezra and company arrive in Jerusalem, dispose of the commissions entrusted to them, and engage in appropriate worship. When the first flurry and activity of the arrival is past, "after these things," the time has come for certain people to bring a serious matter to Ezra's attention.

The entire episode is set in motion by a group called "the officials," who bring an accusation before Ezra. The accusation is that male members from the most important groups in the community—that is, the priests and the Levites, officials and leaders—have married women from the neighboring peoples, here called "the peoples of the lands" (9:2). This phrase, used twice in the section, points to the same groups that had earlier caused fear and hostility among the returnees (Ezra 3:3; 4:4; 6:21). In between the repetition of this expression (vv. 1 and 2), the group is specified with a list. The nations named are a combination of lists found in the book of Deuteronomy (7:1–4 and 23:3–6), with at least one creative addition—the Egyptians. Egyptians do not occur on any lists forbidding intermarriage in the Bible, and they are at least once emphatically included in those with whom ancient Israel may associate (Deut. 23:7). Also, for five of the nationalities, there were in the postexilic period no surviving ethnic groups that could be identified with them. The list is a sampler taken from the very texts in which Ezra is supposed to be an expert. Was this accusation and the recital a kind of test of Ezra's expertise? The effect of the listing is also to tie the experience of the community in Judah closely to that of the people who were on the verge of entering the promised land as it is depicted in Deuteronomy. In its story form, the return from exile in Babylon follows the pattern of the exodus and the liberation from Egypt. Thus, the mention of Egyptians makes sense in its own way and is the first example of the "creative" exegesis that the speakers engage in. Recall that for the community in Judah in the fifth century, the memory of the Babylonian Exile is *the* testimony to what a large group of people understood to be a punishment from God. The loss of land and leadership, of temple and city, the very loss of God's presence had overcome them, according to this perspective, because of their refusal to live a life according to God's will. For such a group, people who look into the past with fear and trembling, it is easy to dream up new fears. One only has to recall what happened before and look at past mistakes in order to understand what the new mistakes are that should be avoided, so that a repetition of the disaster may be avoided also.

Looking at the past is seldom a simple exercise, for one often finds there what one seeks to find. Israel's story includes prescriptions against intermarriage, probably articulated at a period shortly before the downfall of the Northern Kingdom in the eighth century B.C.E. (Deut. 7:1–4; 23:3–6). Israel's story, on the other hand, also includes the presence of "strangers," many of them women who frequently came to the aid of God's people, such as Rahab and Jael, or who were models of faithfulness, such as Ruth. Do these "officials" who come to Ezra not know their own history? Does Ezra, the expert, not know this history? Keep in mind that the orientation of both is motivated by fear more than anything. Perhaps they even reasoned that such a presence of strangers, even when it benefited the community, was precisely what had gone wrong. After all, look at what had happened to them; the same thing could happen again! "The holy seed has mixed itself" (9:2). When such mixing takes place, there is a mixing with other religions as well. Before they would know it, they would be back into old ways of behaving and old ways of idolatry.

The term "holy seed" points to a desire for keeping an ethnic purity, presumably because this would guarantee religious purity. Although the concern about intermarriage is expressed in Deuteronomy, there are other parts of the Torah that counteracted this concern, especially in the many provisions made for the just and loving treatment of strangers. Moreover, the warnings of the prophets who announced the downfall of the community because of its way of life put neither intermarriage nor pure worship in the center, but rather emphasized the need for justice and love toward the neighbor, without which even the purest worship was unacceptable to God. Recall for example the biting words of Jeremiah 7:3–7, a text in which the prophet denounces false trust in the temple as the guarantee of God's presence and exhorts the community to a life of justice and love, especially toward "the alien, the orphan, and the widow" (Jer. 7:6). It was in their common life together as a community that the people failed to live up to the demands God made of them. In the words of Amos, justice had not flowed like waters, nor righteousness like an everflowing stream (Amos 5:24). They had not understood or had not taken seriously the link between the knowledge of God and the knowledge of justice. That lack, according to the prophets, would cause the downfall of the people. By contrast, Ezra 9:1–4 shows the main concern to be the purity of worship to which foreigners are a threat. By intermarrying with foreigners, the people would introduce worship practices that were foreign to the worship of the God of Israel, and God would punish them again; so the reasoning went.

It is easy to look down on what seem to us petty concerns of this group in fifth-century B.C.E. Judah. Yet there is nothing here that is alien to us twentieth-century Christians. We may use different rationales and different appeals, but we may be as intent on defining our identity over against our secular context today as the Jews of Judah were at that time. In essence, we may share the concern of the Jewish community that we will disappear if we do not somehow keep ourselves separate and distinct from the world.

The argument of the officials is effective with Ezra, who engages immediately in acts of mourning (9:3) and sits down in a state of despair comparable to that of Job's companions when they met him after his disaster (Job 2:13). Ezra sits down in shocked silence in the midst of a group with special reverence for the Torah (the most likely interpretation of those "who trembled at the words of the God of Israel," v. 4). Then at three o'clock in the afternoon, the time of the evening sacrifice and proper time of prayer, he begins to pray.

Ezra's Prayer (9:5–15)

A prevailing sense of guilt and responsibility for the current situation pervades the prayer. First, Ezra reviews the past: Captivity and disaster overcame the people because of their "guilt and iniquities" (vv. 6–7). By the use of the first person plural, "we," the speaker draws the present into close identification with the past. This prayer is not so much about then as it is about now. It is *now* that the community is in "utter shame" and slavery (v. 7).

Bluntly the prayer states: "for we are slaves" (v. 9). In the midst of this pitiful situation God has granted a lifeline, with the restoration of temple and city, for "a remnant" (vv. 8–9). And now they are about to derail again!

Then the prayer turns to a rehearsal of prohibitions, mostly from Deuteronomy, all against intermarriage with the indigenous ethnic groups of Canaan and their immediate neighbors. Verse 14 could not state more clearly that fear of repeating the mistakes of the past drives the perspective of this prayer: "Shall we break your commandments again and intermarry with the peoples who practice these abominations? Would you not be angry with us until you destroy us without remnant or survivor?" The next time there will be no lifeline!

Creative Exegesis (10:1–5)

10:1 **While Ezra prayed and made confession, weeping and throwing himself down before the house of God, a very great assembly of men, women, and children gathered to him out of Israel; the people also wept bitterly.** [2] **Shecaniah son of Jehiel, of the descendants of Elam, addressed Ezra, saying, "We have broken faith with our God and have married foreign women from the peoples of the land, but even now there is hope for Israel in spite of this.** [3] **So now let us make a covenant with our God to send away all these wives and their children, according to the counsel of my lord and of those who tremble at the commandment of our God; and let it be done according to the law.** [4] **Take action, for it is your duty, and we are with you; be strong, and do it."** [5] **Then Ezra stood up and made the leading priests, the Levites, and all Israel swear that they would do as had been said. So they swore.**

Ezra does not conduct his activities in private; he makes a public display of his reactions. Naturally, his carrying on attracts a crowd. So the scene is set, and another speech is made to propose a solution to the problem that has been brought to Ezra's attention and for which he has confessed guilt on behalf of the people. In the eyes of some, prayer is not enough, and more pressure is put on Ezra to *do* something about the situation. Praying and weeping are all fine and good, but we need to see some action here. The speaker, one Shecaniah, engages in some more creative exegesis. When folk are afraid and interpreting biblical texts from the midst of their fear, such creativity is not untypical. First, instead of referring to the women as "the daughters of the peoples of the lands," Shecaniah calls them "foreign women" (Ezra 10:2). The Hebrew language makes careful distinctions between categories of people who do not strictly belong to Israel. One category, the most common one, is that of "strangers." Strangers, by our translations often rendered "aliens," were those who came from elsewhere to a clan or a people and lived in their midst. There are more provisions and laws that apply to the stranger than any other category of laws in the Torah, and they cover the spectrum from prohibitions of oppression to exacting love for the stranger (see, for example: Exod. 22:21; 23:9; Lev. 16:29; 19:34; Deut. 1:16; 15:15; 16:19; 21:22; 24:17).

Another, less frequently occurring category of outsiders is "foreigners," those who come from elsewhere and are passing through, who do not intend to stay with the community for whatever reasons. The latter term is what Shecaniah uses to indicate the women who had come from elsewhere and who married into the Jewish community. Clearly, this is not the correct term for those who were living inside the family circle of the Jewish community. Applying the incorrect term to them causes one to think of them as foreigners. Foreigners they are called and foreigners they are. Also, the term anticipates what they will become: They will prove to have been only passing through and will in fact become "foreign women" who were not there to stay with the community. Third, for those who know the law, and who "tremble at the commandment," it may be the better part of wisdom not to assign these women to a category that was as traditionally protected as that of "strangers."

All must be within the law. The solution, sending the women away with their children, must be done "according to the law" (Ezra 10:3). It is interesting to note that there are no laws that provide for this situation. Although there are laws that forbid intermarriage, there are no prescriptions that rearrange families once the marriage has occurred. This is another example of creative exegesis. Such words put special pressure on Ezra, who is after all *the* skilled interpreter and teacher of the law. Do your stuff, Shecaniah urges him. Such manipulation of folk in positions of leadership is a familiar device that many of us will recognize. The leader now has a choice to make, but is in a bind; for if he decides to do other than suggested, it will be seen as going against the law of God. We do not know whether Ezra hesitated; the text does not say. Smoothly, it proceeds to deal with Ezra's acquiescence in the plan.

A Plan Made
and Executed (10:6–44)

10:6 **Then Ezra withdrew from before the house of God, and went to the chamber of Jehohanan son of Eliashib, where he spent the night. He did not eat bread or drink water, for he was mourning over the faithlessness of the exiles. ⁷ They made a proclamation throughout Judah and Jerusalem to all** the returned exiles that they should assemble at Jerusalem, [8] and that if any did not come within three days, by order of the officials and the elders all their property should be forfeited, and they themselves banned from the congregation of the exiles.

[9] Then all the people of Judah and Benjamin assembled at Jerusalem within the three days; it was the ninth month, on the twentieth day of the month. All the people sat in the open square before the house of God, trembling because of this matter and because of the heavy rain. [10] Then Ezra the priest stood up and said to them, "You have trespassed and married foreign women, and so increased the guilt of Israel. [11] Now make confession to the LORD the God of your ancestors, and do his will; separate yourselves from the peoples of the land and from the foreign wives." [12] Then all the assembly answered with a loud voice, "It is so; we must do as you have said. [13] But the people are many, and it is a time of heavy rain; we cannot stand in the open. Nor is this a task for one day or for two, for many of us have transgressed in this matter. [14] Let our officials represent the whole assembly, and let all in our towns who have taken foreign wives come at appointed times, and with them the elders and judges of every town, until the fierce wrath of our God on this account is averted from us." [15] Only Jonathan son of Asahel and Jahzeiah son of Tikvah opposed this, and Meshullam and Shabbethai the Levites supported them.

[16] Then the returned exiles did so. Ezra the priest selected men, heads of families, according to their families, each of them designated by name. On the first day of the tenth month they sat down to examine the matter. [17] By the first day of the first month they had come to the end of all the men who had married foreign women.

Ezra continues to fast, and proclamation is made throughout the province for the returned exiles to come to Jerusalem under threat of forfeiture and banishment (Ezra 10:7–8). Another gathering then takes place, this time planned rather than spontaneous. An assembly takes place to take care of the business of the community. Where our translation has in verse nine "Then all the people . . . assembled," the Hebrew reads literally "men" for "people" (v. 9). It may be erroneous to make the account more inclusive, since only the men were invited, and this was after all men's business. Some interesting shifts have taken place: First there was an assembly of men, women, and children (Ezra 10:1); then a group of the women were defined as "foreign women," and their children were grouped with them (10:2–3); then the suggestion was made to send them away. At the next assembly, the women are absent (10:9).

The ninth month is December, when heavy rains are prone to fall in Jerusalem. So the pathetic crowd listens, shivering, to Ezra's words of denunciation. Ezra has adopted the renaming of the women as "foreign" and twice refers to them as such (10:10–11). The men agree, but ask for some time to do this properly, partly because of the inclement weather and partly because it will take time to sort it all out (Ezra 10:13–15). Only four men oppose the plan, and it is left ambiguous whether they oppose the whole idea or merely the manner of its execution (10:15). Either Jonathan, Jahzeiah, Meshullam, and Shabbethai are the only voices to be heard on the side of the women, or they find the proposal not rigorous enough or too slow. Their mention can only tease our imagination at this point. Their opposition, in any case, has no effect, and the plan is put in motion. A small bureaucracy is put in place to deal with the matter and to sort it all out. After three months, in March of 457 B.C.E., they are ready (Ezra 10:16–17).

There are two familiar ways of dealing with this story that are not helpful. One is to rationalize or excuse it; the other is to condemn it as an example of Jewish narrow-mindedness and rigid understandings of the law. If we rationalize it, the reasoning goes that for this community there was really no alternative but to do what they did. They were so fragile, so much in danger of disappearing and becoming assimilated into the cultures and religions of the time that they had to be extremely strict about who belonged and who did not belong. They were fighting for their survival. But one must keep in mind that the events described here would have taken place a century after the first return in the days of Cyrus and that the population of Judah and Jerusalem had increased since that time. Temple and city walls had been repaired; priesthood and worship were firmly established. It is not clear that there was a great danger to the identity of the community in terms of this small group of women. Would a fairly small group of women have had such a dangerous effect, even if they were all practicing idolatry all the day long? More serious yet, such excuses may function in our own time and context to condone our own practices of exclusion and intolerance toward those who are different in our communities, to the strangers in our midst. The temptation for us might be to let this episode be a model for our version of sending away those who are already on the margin and for defending such actions on biblical grounds.

It is even more damaging if we engage in wholesale condemnation of the episode, not because it was inhumane or cruel or against God's will, but because there would be something particularly Jewish about it. This path is a dangerous one to tread for Christians who have a long history of persecuting the very people they condemn because of their supposed rigid and intolerant attitudes. In particular, it should be clear how dangerous a path this is in light of the Holocaust, which among other things was also the logical end of centuries of Christian persecution of the Jews. Such an interpretation literally has murderous implications, and there will be murderers around to spell them out. In addition, if we look at the process of reasoning present in the text, we discover that the law, far from being rigidly appropriated, is applied creatively. The problem of the officials and Ezra is not rigidity.

Look again at what is going on. The leaders of the community are afraid, and they cause Ezra and the entire community to be afraid. They are afraid that God will punish them by taking away the little they have regained of land, city, temple, and community if they do not obey God's will. Their fear causes them to look for possible failings and for groups that might be the cause of these failings. Identity and concerns about who belonged to the community, to "Israel," had been in the air since the first exiles returned in the days of Cyrus. Fear looks for a scapegoat. The officials and Ezra locate a scapegoat in the group of women who have been taken into marriage by the Jews (Ezra 9:2). This is considered such a grave breach of God's law that a group of possibly 400–500 people, 111 women and their children, were banished from the community (Ezra 10:18–44). Many of them, especially those who had no family circle to return to, would perish because they lacked the necessary means to sustain their existence. There is no excuse for it, and there is no precedent for it in the laws anywhere. Rather, the laws in the Torah demand protection and care for strangers in all the different law codes.

It is striking in this section that the names of women are missing. It is after all the women who are held responsible, for they are the ones who are banished. The males who had married them are given full publicity. Was this publicity their punishment? Why are they not the ones banished, since they were responsible for the marriages? The males experience hardship for sure, especially insofar as a separation from wife and children would affect them emotionally. But the brunt of the sacrifice is borne by the women and children, the weakest members of the group—the ones without a name and a voice. There is nothing good about this, and it is an example of cowardly and condemnable behavior on the part of the male members of the community. There is also nothing particularly Jewish about it. It is still true in our society and in our religious communities that women and children receive the brunt of the violence we perpetrate on one another. Our own religious communities are as expert as was the community in Judah in using biblical texts "creatively" to exclude and even banish from our midst those we judge to practice "abominations."

In his speech to Ezra, Shecaniah proclaims that "even now there is hope for Israel in spite of this" (Ezra 10:2). Shecaniah spoke truth in spite of himself. For there was indeed hope for Israel, and there is hope for the church. Like Israel, if we look at our past, we see a history littered with guilt and iniquities. We see a church that instituted an anti-Jewish tradition of stupendous virulence; a church that invented the inquisition and perpetrated witch hunts; a church that went on crusades, that participated in slavery and defended it on biblical grounds; a church that at all times in all places continued the sins of the ancestors by denying women their human dignity and equality before God. Yet in spite of this, even now there is hope. For our hope is not built on the church. Our hope resides in a gracious God and in our teacher Jesus Christ. There is no hope in the "letter of the law," no matter how creatively interpreted. Our hope is in the living word of the living God who addresses us anew in each age to meet the particular challenges that encounter us there.

3. Reviving the Stones
Nehemiah 1—7

The progress of the narrative named for Nehemiah is similar to that of Ezra. There is a return of exiles to Jerusalem and a building project that runs into considerable difficulties. Both the return and the restoration of the city walls take place under the leadership of Nehemiah. Then follow attempts at rebuilding the community under the guidance of the Torah as read by Ezra. Celebrations and further efforts to restore life and worship in Jerusalem close the book. The Torah moves to the front in Nehemiah as the major document that guides the religious and social decisions of the community.

The first seven chapters of Nehemiah concern themselves with another return of Jewish exiles from Persia to Jerusalem, this time under the leadership of Nehemiah. These chapters are presented in the first person singular, so that one views the events from the perspective of Nehemiah. The objective of the return is to rebuild the city walls of Jerusalem. This effort is complicated by hostilities toward Nehemiah and his rebuilding efforts from individuals in the region (Nehemiah 1—3). The building of the city walls continues, but takes place under duress (Nehemiah 4). Another complication in the story arises because of mistreatment in the community from neighbor to neighbor on account of severe taxation (Nehemiah 5). A second wave of plots against the repair work is not successful, and the work on the walls is completed. The set of chapters closes with a list of families that is largely identical to the list in the second chapter of Ezra (Nehemiah 6—7).

A BROKEN HOME
Nehemiah 1—3

A Question of Survival (1:1–3)

1:1 **The words of Nehemiah son of Hacaliah. In the month of Chislev, in the twentieth year, while I was in Susa the capital, ² one of my brothers, Hanani,**

came with certain men from Judah; and I asked them about the Jews that
survived, those who had escaped the captivity, and about Jerusalem. [3] They
replied, "The survivors there in the province who escaped captivity are in
great trouble and shame; the wall of Jerusalem is broken down, and its gates
have been destroyed by fire."

The first seven chapters of Nehemiah are written in the "I" form. As with
the memoir of Ezra, scholars suggest that an actual memoir of Nehemiah
is the source for this material. The effect of presenting the story in the first
person singular is that we see everything and everybody from Nehemiah's
perspective. To get a better picture of the situation, of people and events,
it may be necessary at times to set this viewpoint aside and ask why
Nehemiah tells the story in this particular way.

The time of the opening episode is November/December in 446 or 445
B.C.E., if the year is that of King Artaxerxes I. Oddly, the name of the king
is missing, and the phrase reads merely "in the twentieth year." We return
to this omission below. There is again some chronological confusion, if we
take the time indicator of Nehemiah 2:1 into account, but we will simply
assume that some time around this date a Jew called Nehemiah heard rumors at the king's court about the situation back home. The period is well
over a century later than that of the conquest of Jerusalem, and it seems
odd to ask about "those who had escaped the captivity," for surely no one
of that generation would still be alive. Once more, we do well not to be too
literal-minded and may surmise that the question relates to the population
of Jerusalem, both in respect to the descendants of the people who were
never taken to Babylon and of those who had returned from exile. The
news in any case is dire. Things are not going at all well in the community
in Judah, for the city walls are in a state of disrepair and ruin.

Perhaps repairs on the walls had begun at an earlier time and the work
that had been completed has now fallen in disrepair, so that the city might
as well be without walls altogether. Recall that the letter from Artaxerxes
quoted in Ezra 4:17–22 contained an order not to rebuild the city; moreover, the recipients of that letter caused the work in which the inhabitants
of Jerusalem were engaged to cease (Ezra 4:23). Although Artaxerxes' directives are quoted in the book of Ezra in the context of restoring the sanctuary, the letter clearly concerns rebuilding the city. The accusers state
unequivocally, "they are finishing the walls and repairing the foundations"
(Ezra 4:12). It is possible then that the exchange of documents in Ezra 4 re-
flects partial work on the city walls that was halted by force at one time. Half-
finished work is naturally more vulnerable to decay and accidental damage.

We may not be overly familiar with city walls or know about their importance in the past, but perhaps some of us have visited cities in Europe of which the walls have been preserved. People in the United States are most likely acquainted with the forts that were used in the hostilities with the Native American peoples in previous centuries. Cities such as we find in the Bible were walled and functioned in some way like a fort. Inside the walls, the life of the citizenry took place according to the laws of the time; outside the walls, life was much more precarious and uncertain. Walls had gates that were closed at a certain time at night, not to be opened again until daylight. Soldiers and watchmen would patrol the walls of the city to keep an eye on things during the night. City walls were wide enough to walk on. Today, one can still take a walk on the walls around the city called "Old Jerusalem" in Israel, a city that goes back to the Middle Ages. Such structures were a necessity in the days of Ezra and Nehemiah to foster economic and social stability. Without the walls there could not be a flourishing city. I have already spoken about the close connection between the city and the temple as a symbol of holiness and a sign of the presence of God with the community. The walls thus functioned also to enable the city of God, Zion, to be an effective symbol of God's presence, and the absence of the walls or their state of disrepair betokened a sense of abandonment by God.

Nehemiah's Prayer (1:4–11)

Nehemiah's dismay does not come as a surprise. Like Ezra before him, at the news of mixed marriages Nehemiah sits down and weeps, mourns, fasts, and prays. The language used in Nehemiah's prayer is stereotypical and borrows heavily from the book of Deuteronomy. Nevertheless, the prayer is worth our attention, because it provides a brief review of essential faith concepts. Nehemiah addresses God in the most majestic terms possible: "O LORD God of heaven, the great and awesome God," and at the same time establishes a close connection between this God and God's people, "those who love him and keep his commandments" (Neh. 1:5). God is allied with these folk in covenant and steadfast love. In addition, when God is described or invoked in such lofty terms, it may be to remind the community of God's particular care for the downtrodden (see Deut. 10:17–19, for example). By implication, the prayer emphasizes a characteristic of God that will make it more likely for God to pay attention to the pitiful state of the community in Jerusalem.

The plea for attention thus follows naturally on the lofty address: "Let your ear be attentive and your eyes open" (Neh. 1:6). Fervent requests for

God's attention characterize prayers in the Bible that bemoan the·lamentable condition of an individual and/or the community. Numerous psalms witness to the importance of this petition. (See Pss. 5:1; 13:3; 17:1, 6; 31:2; 39:12; 45:10; 54:2; 55:1; 71:2; 80:1; 86:1, 6; 88:2; 102:2; 140:6; 141:1; 143:1.) Often such a plea will be followed by a description of the particular distress of the one who utters the prayer. Sometimes this type of prayer also includes a confession of sin; sometimes it has a protestation of innocence instead. Nehemiah skips over the particulars of the condition and offers an elaborate confession (Neh. 1:6–7). Remember that the conquest of Jerusalem, the Babylonian Exile, and its aftermath were understood by many to be a result of the community's failure to live according to God's will. As is characteristic of this type of prayer in the Bible, the sins mentioned lack all precision and are described in the most general terms: "We have sinned against you. Both I and my family have sinned. We have offended you deeply, failing to keep the commandments, the statutes, and the ordinances that you commanded" (Neh. 1:6–7). Words for sin, failure, and offense predominate and fail to find a concrete form. The general tone is all the more striking in view of the particularity of the distress, the broken state of the walls and the city in Judah. Rather than stressing the broken walls, the prayer lifts up the broken commandments. In this manner the text anticipates the central place of the Torah, a theme that will predominate in the rebuilding of the community once the city walls are repaired (Neh. 8—10); at that time the focus on the Torah will also cause a sensitivity to shortcomings and a mood of repentance (Neh. 8:9 and 9:32–36).

In Nehemiah's prayer the Torah is referred to with the words "your servant Moses." Twice in a short span this phrase is repeated, once to conclude the confession, and once to open a renewed request (Neh. 1:7–8). Verses 8–10 begin with a plea to God and close with a repeat of the entreaty for attention in verse 6, while adding a variation. The plea this time is based on God's promise of the past: Faithlessness on the part of the community would have dire consequences, but repentance (v. 9: "if you return to me") would cause gracious action on God's part. In this section especially, the prayer leans heavily on language from the book of Deuteronomy. The city is not called Jerusalem but "the place at which I have chosen to establish my name" (v. 9), a reference typical for Deuteronomy. Verse 10 establishes the basis for God's promise as relational and historical: "They are your servants and your people, whom you redeemed by your great power and your strong hand."

The prayer ends with a turn toward the personal, when Nehemiah prays for success (v. 11). Throughout the prayer the word "servant" is repeated to indicate the relation of Nehemiah and the community to God. Such repetitions underscore the importance of a certain idea in a text. Nehemiah calls himself a servant, puts himself in the context of other servants, that is, the people of God, and also relates himself and his community to the servant par excellence, Moses. The word *servant* frames the person and the community in a strong relation of loyalty to God rather than in a posture of servitude. Nehemiah thus describes himself as oriented toward God, and he does this in the context of his community, which is likewise oriented. In verse 11 Nehemiah refers to himself twice as God's servant. We will see that it is crucial for Nehemiah to set himself in a strong relationship to God and God's covenanted community, the Jews. The prayer itself, strongly based in the Torah, and the emphatic self-identification as God's servant should leave no one in doubt as to where Nehemiah's loyalties lie. With the recall of Moses as God's servant, the expression gains its greatest force since Moses functioned as the model of loyalty. But God also is held to loyalty in this prayer, by the recall of the covenant, the promises, and the faithful action of God in the past. By strong implication, this prayer is a cry for help. The details are left to the understanding ear of God mentioned in the repeated appeal of verses 5–6 and 11.

The plea for success with which the prayer ends leaves open what Nehemiah intends to undertake. It is clear, however, that his plans are risky and somehow relate to the person called "this man." The very last words of the prayer sound an almost ominous note: "and grant him mercy in the sight of this man!" (Neh. 1:11). The words "this man" provide a strong contrast with the term "your servant(s)." Nehemiah and the community stand in close relation to God, unlike the king of Persia who remains unnamed and untitled in this chapter. This omission is especially obvious in the first verse, but throughout the chapter the absence of this reference stands in striking contrast to the emphatic naming of King Cyrus in Ezra 1. Here, Artaxerxes does not appear until the final phrase of chapter 1, and even then not by name but by title only: "the king."

The final notation, "At the time, I was cupbearer to the king" (v. 11), puts Nehemiah squarely in the context of his present reality. Nehemiah, God's servant, is also a servant of the king of Persia, "this man" who exercises total power over his life and the life of his community. This reality has been mentioned obliquely only, but is nevertheless the overriding factor of unpredictable power in Nehemiah's life. Unlike God, the king cannot be appealed to on the basis of past promises and past actions or because of covenant loyalties and steadfast love. The king is "this man" (v. 11), that is to say, a mere man, and not one of God's servants, not one of Nehemiah's community. Yet "this man" happens to be *the man*, the one who holds the life of Nehemiah and his folk in the palm of his hand, on whose generous impulses will hang the outcome of Nehemiah's efforts.

Also, Nehemiah declares his own position in relation to the king with his words. "Cupbearer" may not sound like much of a position to us, but it was in actuality an influential and powerful office. And in this fact, that Nehemiah holds office at the king of Persia's court, lies a painful and conflictual aspect of Nehemiah's reality. He is a Jew, he cares deeply about his community, he feels himself to be loyal to his God, but he is employed by and hence beholden to the foreign power that dominates the life of his community both in Persia and in Judah. On "this man" depends the welfare of what he sets out to undertake. To an extent, Nehemiah represents the king's power from the perspective of his people. Nehemiah's authority must have been viewed as at least partly compromised by this connection to the foreign overlord. His position is less secure than Ezra's, so he continuously protests his virtue and impeccable behavior toward his kindred, pleading with God to be on his side.

Dinner Table Talk (2:1–10)

> 2:1 **In the month of Nisan, in the twentieth year of King Artaxerxes, when wine was served him, I carried the wine and gave it to the king. Now, I had never been sad in his presence before.** [2] **So the king said to me, "Why is your face sad, since you are not sick? This can only be sadness of the heart." Then I was very much afraid.** [3] **I said to the king, "May the king live forever! Why should my face not be sad, when the city, the place of my ancestors' graves, lies waste, and its gates have been destroyed by fire?"** [4] **Then the king said to me, "What do you request?" So I prayed to the God of heaven.** [5] **Then I said to the king, "If it pleases the king, and if your servant has found favor with you, I ask that you send me to Judah, to the city of my ancestors' graves, so that I may rebuild it."** [6] **The king said to me (the queen also was sitting beside him), "How long will you be gone, and when will you return?" So it pleased the king to send me, and I set him a date.**

In line with Nehemiah's indirect approach to things, he draws attention to himself while performing his task by a change in his usual demeanor. It was most likely not considered prudent to show one's royal employer the true state of one's feelings. The scene that unfolds in chapter 2 provides a close-up of the occasion. The flow of time is halted as the king and his servant converse at the dinner table, and an intimate, almost cozy scene is presented. The king, is concerned about the unusual mien of his cupbearer, and engages in an interested conversation with him. Yet the overt domesticity belies the danger Nehemiah believes himself to be in and the enormous decisions being made. Two remarks, presented as asides, give away the true state of affairs: first, Nehemiah states his fear. Not only is he afraid, he is "very much afraid" (v. 2). The king has already seen through him and knows the cause of his sadness to be of the spirit, or heart, rather than the body. Next, he sends a prayer to God, no doubt silently, before he makes his actual request. It was most likely considered to be offensive to show one's feelings to a monarch, let alone make exorbitant demands with a long face. Who knows what the king will do! Servants have been sent away empty-handed, been exiled, even been killed for less.

When the king asks for the reason for his sadness, it is crucial that Nehemiah chooses his words with extreme care. He needs to go to the heart of the matter without giving further offense. After the appropriate phrase of good wishes for the king, Nehemiah proceeds to answer the king's question with a question of his own. How could he be other than sad, when things go so badly for his city? The reference seems straightforward, but we notice that he refers to Jerusalem as "the city, the place of my ancestors' graves," rather than by its name (Neh. 2:3). When he voices his request to go and rebuild the city, he names Judah, but again not Jerusalem, calling it instead "the city of my ancestors' graves" (Neh. 2:5). If this is the same king as the one who considered Jerusalem to be a hotbed of rebellion and sedition, whose letter is quoted in Ezra 4:17–22, we do not wonder about Nehemiah's fear and his reticence. Nehemiah relates the city directly to himself and his family by his reference, appealing to the personal rather than the political dimension.

No one is fooled, of course, least of all the king, as to the true location and name of the place of Nehemiah's origin, but Nehemiah achieves his goal of presenting his case in just the right light. The king appears more worried about a lengthy absence of his cupbearer than an uprising in Judah. Royal permission is given, supplies are provided, as well as letters for the appropriate officials. Unlike Ezra, who had been ashamed to ask for military protection, Nehemiah goes to Judah accompanied by soldiers (Neh. 2:9). This reality again emphasizes Nehemiah's close relation to the Persian court.

One fact mentioned here by allusion only is that the king appoints Nehemiah as governor of Judah. In Nehemiah 5:14, the text conveys that at this time Nehemiah indeed became the governor. That reality is hidden in the phrase "So it pleased the king to send me" (Neh. 2:6). Again, not all is as straightforward and clear as it may seem at first glance. Why would

Nehemiah not mention his governorship at this point? Nehemiah's relation to the Persian court is understated, most likely because of the possible conflict that this relation could create for him in relation to his own
community. Foreign conquerors often establish one of the conquered nation's own to rule on their behalf. During the Second World War in the
country of my origin, The Netherlands, one of the most hated figures was
the Dutch administrator put in place by the Germans to govern the nation. Such people are generally not regarded fondly. Nehemiah, in any
case, sees his appointment not as a reason for pride and mentions it only
in passing and in a context of self-defense (Neh. 5:14–19).

The end of this episode sees the new governor on his way to Jerusalem
already in conflict with other authorities in the region. This is the first time
that we hear the names of "Sanballat the Horonite and Tobiah the Ammonite" (Neh. 2:10) and it will not be the last. So we may as well make
ourselves familiar with these two. Sanballat was the governor of Samaria;
Tobiah was probably in a similar position in Ammon, to the East. They
never receive the title of their office in this text and are from the beginning in a hostile position to Nehemiah. Their activities cause Nehemiah
and the community in Judah no end of trouble. Is Nehemiah perhaps all
too eager to distance himself from other governors? He is not like them
because, as the text phrases it, he is one who has come "to seek the welfare
of the people of Israel" (Neh. 2:10). The welfare of the Persian realm rather
than that of the indigenous people was more likely to be an appropriate
concern of a governor.

A Troubled Arrival (2:11–20)

2:17 Then I said to them, "You see the trouble we are in, how Jerusalem lies
in ruins with its gates burned. Come, let us rebuild the wall of Jerusalem, so
that we may no longer suffer disgrace." [18] I told them that the hand of my
God had been gracious upon me, and also the words that the king had spoken to me. Then they said, "Let us start building!" So they committed themselves to the common good. [19] But when Sanballat the Horonite and Tobiah
the Ammonite official, and Geshem the Arab heard of it, they mocked and
ridiculed us, saying, "What is this that you are doing? Are you rebelling
against the king?" [20] Then I replied to them, "The God of heaven is the one
who will give us success, and we his servants are going to start building; but
you have no share or claim or historic right in Jerusalem."

In 2:11 Jerusalem is named for the first time. Nehemiah has come to the
city that symbolizes the presence of God, but in its present state it also

symbolizes uncertainty over the continuation of the community that calls itself God's people. First, Nehemiah goes on an inspection tour to investigate the extent of the damage. He wants no one to interfere or ask questions at this point and goes out on his own to become more clear about the necessary repairs. Twice he states the lack of knowledge of his activities on the part of the community (vv. 12 and 16), and, finally, he is ready to reveal his plan.

As if to make up for earlier reticence, Nehemiah now uses the name of Jerusalem where it no longer seems necessary. Surely his audience knows what city he is referring to (2:17). It is, however, not just any city, but *Jerusalem* that lies in ruins and *Jerusalem* that needs rebuilding. The last word in the section is also *Jerusalem*. Now the name that had been held back comes to the fore. Nehemiah has only to convince the community of the favor of God and king toward him and they are ready to begin building. But no sooner has the work started than new troubles arise. Sanballat and Tobiah, joined by an Arab ruler, Geshem, begin their campaign of mockery and terrorization. Like Sanballat and Tobiah, Geshem lacks any reference to his office and title. The threat the trio utters relates the community to the power of the king. Nehemiah's reply does not directly deny the charge of possible rebellion. Rather, he affirms the most important relationship of the people, which is to their God, and their dependence on God's power. At the same time, he distances the three men from this relation as well as from a possible relation to Jerusalem. We, he says in so many words, are under God's aegis, unlike you. You, who are under the aegis of the king, are not a part of us, and you do not belong here in the city of God, Jerusalem. Temporarily at least, the enemies are silenced, but they will return. In the meantime, the building of the walls progresses, and chapter 3 presents a list of the families involved in the work.

Families at Work (3:1–32)

Another list we may sigh! As we know already, lists are the cement that holds the structure of Ezra-Nehemiah together. We do not need to read all the names presented here, but even at a glance we may get the feeling of righting the balance a bit. The text had begun to tilt too far in the direction of Nehemiah. Now the emphasis returns to the community who did the actual work and whose hands restored the gates and the walls. A long parade, and an important one, with details regarding who worked where and which section was repaired by whom, marches here before our eyes. It is in the end the community that needs to put its hands to work, the community that needs to face the hostilities of outsiders, and the community that needs to be reestablished in its relation to God.

Before the families and their activities are listed, the high priest Eliashib is said to consecrate one of the gates (Neh. 3:1). The consecration of something as secular as a wall or a gate once more points us in the direction of close connections between temple and wall, between the city as living space for the populace and as holy place at the same time. For the covenant community, the secular and the religious world are not sharply separated. When the entire work is accomplished, the whole wall will be dedicated with religious ceremonies (Neh. 12:27–43).

A WEAPON IN THE HAND
Nehemiah 4

Insults Hurled (4:1–3)

> 4:1 Now when Sanballat heard that we were building the wall, he was angry and greatly enraged, and he mocked the Jews. [2] He said in the presence of his associates and of the army of Samaria, "What are these feeble Jews doing? Will they restore things? Will they sacrifice? Will they finish it in a day? Will they revive the stones out of the heaps of rubbish—and burned ones at that?" [3] Tobiah the Ammonite was beside him, and he said, "That stone wall they are building—any fox going up on it would break it down!"

This is the third time that hostility is recorded regarding the building efforts in Jerusalem. At each mention, the opposition of Sanballat and his associates becomes more elaborate. What was initially introduced as "displeasure" (2:10) and eventually became suspicious questioning (2:19) now turns into insults and mockery. In contrast to hostile plotters at the time of the temple building, this group makes no attempt to work an intrigue with the Persian ruler (see Ezra 4:6–24). Rather, Sanballat and friends aim their words directly at the community that occupies itself with the work; their speech is intended to demoralize and undermine trust both in the people's own capacity and in the capability of their leader, Nehemiah. A series of derisive questions underlines the uselessness of the endeavor: Will they restore? sacrifice? finish? revive? These questions are prefaced by the reference to "these feeble Jews." The assumed reply to the questions is "Of course not!" The place is dead, and the community is so feeble, it might as well be dead. There is no reviving this dead place. For good measure, Tobiah comments that even as notoriously light-footed an animal as a fox will cause the structure to collapse.

We might not consider the tone and words of Sanballat and Tobiah serious threats, but mockery can be very effective both as an aggressive and defensive weapon. During the Second World War the Nazis mocked and ridiculed their Jewish victims to increase the campaign of terror against them. Conversely, occupied communities and groups of victims used their own ridicule of the tyrant in narrative, picture, and song. What works on the one hand to further oppression can be used on the other hand to cut oppression down to size and engender a measure of hope.

To how great a degree mockery was encountered as a painful experience in the ancient covenant community is evident from a number of psalms. "All who see me mock at me," cries the psalmist, "they stare and gloat over me" (Ps. 22:7, 17). Both for the individual and the community, taunts are among the sharpest grief recounted in these prayers: "My adversaries taunt me"; "You have made us . . . a laughingstock among the peoples"; "Insults have broken my heart"; "You have made us the scorn of our neighbors; our enemies laugh among themselves"; "All day long my enemies taunt me; those who deride me use my name for a curse" (Pss. 42:10; 44:14; 69:20; 80:6; 102:8).

A Prayer for Vengeance (4:4–5)

4:4 **Hear, O our God, for we are despised; turn their taunt back on their own heads, and give them over as plunder in a land of captivity. ⁵ Do not cover their guilt, and do not let their sin be blotted out from your sight; for they have hurled insults in the face of the builders.**

In the face of the hostility coming from the faction in Samaria, Nehemiah prays for the undoing of the enemies and their mockery. The style used here is that of traditional prayers for vengeance in the Hebrew Bible. Requests for vengeance are generally frowned on by a Christian community that is mindful of Jesus' requirement to pray *for* enemies and to turn the other cheek. We may skip over prayers in the Bible that ask for the destruction of the enemy and consign them to the less acceptable expressions of beliefs present in the Old Testament. I suggest that we take into account the possible appropriateness of such prayers. It is not *always* appropriate to turn the other cheek; in the case of abuse, for example, few would counsel victims to follow this route. Neither is it *always* appropriate to ask God to destroy the enemy. But there may be moments when a prayer for vengeance is the only thing that fits.

There are certainly times that the believers in ancient Israel ask God to destroy those who have hurt them, who have caused them anger and despair. The benefit to be derived from such articulations of human anger is first the recognition of the fact that such expressions are part of human nature. It is human to feel angry and vengeful, and it may be more productive to own such feelings than to deny having them. Second, human beings can become stuck in their feelings of revenge and retaliation to the degree that it paralyzes them. Perhaps one way to become unstuck is to let go of such feelings in prayer. And last, prayers of vengeance are words, and such words are after all in themselves not destructive. There is nothing noble or good about anger and desire for vengeance, but we might do worse perhaps than putting such feelings into God's care.

Not long ago, I heard a speaker give powerful witness to such a process of moving from feelings of vengeance to understanding and forgiveness. She was a mother whose seven-year-old daughter had been kidnapped and later murdered. While the search for her daughter was going on, in the early days after the kidnapping, the mother expressed her feelings of rage and desire for vengeance toward the perpetrator one night in the strongest terms to her husband, as she reported to the audience. Then, almost as soon as the words of vengeance were out of her mouth, she experienced an equally strong feeling that this should not be her attitude. She felt that even the offender deserved the grace of God, and through long months of agonized waiting she practiced forgiveness toward him in prayer. By the time she was contacted by the perpetrator, she was able to reach him so that he opened his heart to her. The body of her child was eventually recovered and the offender apprehended. This mother stood before her audience to testify against the death penalty and on behalf of a consideration of all human beings as God's creatures, even those who commit crimes. Her process was one of letting go of her feelings of vengeance, which might have been more difficult had she not expressed herself quite openly at first. Her words of desire for retribution that initially expressed her emotions were replaced by strong, faith-filled considerations of compassion.

Nehemiah voices his feelings in a prayer, rather than returning taunts to Sanballat and his efforts. In this way he does not up the ante, but relieves his pent-up feelings and puts them in God's safekeeping. Also, recall that Nehemiah himself is a representative of the Persian government. In prayers such as these, he distances himself from other representatives who put themselves squarely in opposition to the builders in Jerusalem.

Nehemiah, a Jew himself, must walk the difficult tightrope of being *for* Persia and at the same time *for* the Jews. One way to do this is to put as much distance between himself and other representatives of the empire, especially if these are not forthcoming with support for the building plans.

Repair and Defense (4:6–23)

4:21 **So we labored at the work, and half of them held the spears from break of dawn until the stars came out.** [22] **I also said to the people at that time, "Let every man and his servant pass the night inside Jerusalem, so that they may be a guard for us by night and may labor by day."** [23] **So neither I nor my brothers nor my servants nor the men of the guard who followed me ever took off our clothes; each kept his weapon in his right hand.**

Verses 7–20 tell of planned assaults from the side of the taunters as well as counter measures taken by Nehemiah to foil these plans. The report is that Sanballat and others became more and more enraged and planned to stop the work by force. These reports in themselves have a debilitating effect. Both the duress of the work itself and the pressure of perceived antagonism cause a flagging of spirits, and Nehemiah must both inspire them anew and arm them against eventual assault.

When we consider the entire episode, it may strike us that nothing actually happens in terms of hostile attempts to stop the work from progressing. There is a *report* of mockery and taunting in Samaria, but it is not clear how this report reached Nehemiah and the folks in Jerusalem. Subsequently, there are several accounts of Sanballat and Tobiah's anger. In verse 7 these two have swelled into a crowd, so that it sounds as if enemies surround Jerusalem and Nehemiah on all sides: "all plotted together to come and fight against Jerusalem" (Neh. 4:8). Henceforth these are called "our enemies" in the chapter. But there is no report of an approach by these "enemies," nor of an actual assault. The enemy never came!

Is Nehemiah taking measures in view of a real threat, or is the threat actual but minimal and blown out of proportion both by Nehemiah, for his own reasons, and by the community out of fear? Remember that Nehemiah needed to prove himself and that the community had reason to be afraid and uncertain in light of past interference and failure. It is certain that by the end of the episode Nehemiah has proven himself to be a stalwart defender of the community. Just in case there were people who mistrusted his leadership, who questioned his championship of the community in Jerusalem in view of his Persian allegiance, who perhaps doubted his courage and his persistence, all such questions have now been put to rest. So who can blame Nehemiah if he fanned the fires of rumors a little and made the threat to be somewhat bigger than it was in reality?

The very notion of arming themselves against a possible attack may have provided a rallying point for the community. The "feeble Jews" of Sanballat's mockery are ready to defend their project and the community. The verb used in Hebrew for holding the weapons is the same one that occurs multiple times in the previous chapter for the repairing of the walls. The goal of the workers is to *strengthen* or repair the walls of the city, so it may once more become a city to live in and a worthy symbol of God's presence. Once, the return of the exiles was aided by a "*strengthening* of the hands" in the days of king Cyrus (Ezra 1:6); now the *strengthening* of the hands for the task of rebuilding is accomplished by the *holding* of weaponry, a more symbolic than realistic tool of self-defense, intended to boost the morale of the workers more than to ward off an actual assault.

THE COST OF TAXATION
Nehemiah 5

A Troubled Community (5:1–13)

5:1 Now there was a great outcry of the people and of their wives against their Jewish kin. 2 For there were those who said, "With our sons and our daughters, we are many; we must get grain, so that we may eat and stay alive." 3 There were also those who said, "We are having to pledge our fields, our vineyards, and our houses in order to get grain during the famine." 4 And there were those who said, "We are having to borrow money on our fields and vineyards to pay the king's tax. 5 Now our flesh is the same as that of our kindred; our children are the same as their children; and yet we are forcing our sons and daughters to be slaves, and some of our daughters have been ravished; we are powerless, and our fields and vineyards now belong to others."

How much Nehemiah needed to be in good standing with the community in Judah becomes clear from this episode. No sooner do the troubles caused by "outsiders" seem under control than inside problems come to the fore. Chapter 5 provides a unique insight into a troubled and divided community. Until this point, the Jews have been shown as a fragile but united group bound together by its industrious eagerness to rebuild the city, beset only by troubles from outside. Now it is revealed that far more is amiss here than can be accounted for by broken walls. These folk are in "great trouble and shame," as the report had it when Nehemiah was still at the court in Persia (Neh. 1:3), because they are a broken community. As we ponder the difficulties brought to Nehemiah's attention in this chapter, it may help to sketch the administrative organization of the province to arrive at more clarity about the chain of authority and about major stress factors in the setup.

The Persian administration of a province like Judah consisted of a governor, Persian or Jewish, who was responsible to a satrap, an administrative appointee in charge of a larger region (Ezra 8:36). Nehemiah was a governor, and so was his opponent Sanballat. The Persian provincial administration was formed by the governor, his family members, and a team of officials, mostly Jewish but also including foreigners. Nehemiah 5:17 refers to this latter group. A tax had to be raised from the province to finance the governor's court and his administration.

Next in authority were two groups of self-government over the Jewish community: the elders or heads of families, in Nehemiah called the "nobles" (Neh. 5:7); and the college of priests, consisting of priests, Levites, and other temple personnel, all directly responsible to the high priest. This complex web of authorities shows possibilities of conflict and instability and a clear need for dependable leadership in important positions such as those of the governorship. Yet the position of governor was also potentially filled with tension and instability, especially if the appointee were a Jew who would be obligated to balance the needs of the community with the demands of the empire.

A destabilizing factor in the political and economical situation was taxation. Large empires are expensive. All the administrative courts needed to be financed, and large sums had to be raised from the communities in the provinces. We may imagine that a portion of the taxes went directly to the royal court and the maintenance of the army. Other portions would be allotted to the lower administrative courts including the groups that represented self-government. These taxes did not fall from the trees but had to be raised by individuals, local officials who doubtless sought to be repaid in turn for their trouble. "Tax collectors" did not get a bad reputation for nothing. Moreover, those who could not raise the money for their taxes would have to borrow the money to be paid back with interest. The largest burden for the taxation fell on groups with the least amount of power, the farmers and poorer parts of the population. Such was more or less the situation we must keep in mind when considering this passage in Nehemiah 5.

There are basically three groups that are issuing a complaint: those who have too many mouths to feed in view of a food shortage; those who must jeopardize their fields and property in order to obtain food; and those who complain about the need to borrow money in view of the demand for the Persian tax, here called "the king's tax" (v. 4). The general complaint is loss of goods and children. It was lawfully permissible in those times for creditors to seize property and family members as pledges on a debt (see 2 Kings 4:1–7). Demanding interest on a loan was, however, against the law (Lev. 25:36–37). The entire outcry is related to taxation, directly or indirectly, and the main complaint of verse 5 is that these actions are perpetrated within the community by "kinfolk." It is one thing to endure the hostility of outsiders; it is a far greater burden to suffer oppression from one's own. It is telling that precisely at this point not only "the people" voice their protest but that "the wives" are included (5:1). The women had a clear stake in all of this; household and children are both in jeopardy, two areas that concern women directly.

What is amiss here goes to the root of the faith of ancient Israel: A people that saw itself in alliance with a God who was the maker of "justice for the poor" (Ps. 140:12) was required to emulate this posture in its common life. Injustice, the privileging of the rich to the disadvantage of the poor, goes against the calling of this covenant community, and one prophet after another had taken the people and its leaders to task for not living up to this calling. In the eighth century B.C.E., Amos, well-known for holding the society accountable for divisions between rich and poor, had accused the well-to-do of bringing down "a reign of violence" on the poor (Amos 6:3). The God of the Bible is so opposed to the violence that victimizes the poor that the worship of a community that perpetrates this injustice is declared unacceptable. In speech after speech, the prophets had attempted to convince the people of this truth. According to Isaiah, God had no pleasure in any of the rites of worship and would not pay attention to the people's prayers, since the same hands that they stretch out to God are "full of blood" (Isa. 1:15). In Judah of the restoration period, it looks as if history is repeating itself. A city with walls intact and temple in working order will still not be a home and a symbol of God's presence if the injustice described in Nehemiah 5 prevails.

Nehemiah is not at all pleased. He talks to the group he considers responsible for this situation, the nobles and the officials, charges them with taking interest, berates them for selling their "own kin," and orders them to restore what they have taken, including the interest. Who are these nobles and officials? Are they the same people who so boldly repaired the wall, weapon in hand? Chapters 4 and 5 make an interesting contrast. In chapter 4, the "nobles and officials" are among those directly addressed by

Nehemiah in connection with repairing the wall and defending the effort. In chapter 5 they are again addressed by Nehemiah; this time he upbraids them for their unjust treatment of members of the community. Nehemiah, who is himself lending money to those who need it, exhorts this group sternly to restore what was taken (Neh. 5:11). He has gained enough authority and credibility to demand restoration of goods and persons taken in pledge for loans, and he procures agreement from the group that had perpetrated the offense.

We have seen how strongly Nehemiah has allied himself with his community. Now the moment has arrived when he must take a stand *against* some in the community in order to support others. The ones who need his support are the weakest and most vulnerable among the population. Nehemiah takes a clear stand against abuse of this group by those who are in leadership positions. In doing so, he separates himself from his own class, for the perpetrators of the injustices were people in the administration and moneylenders, of whom Nehemiah is one by his own admission (v. 10). The leaders in the community are ostensibly in accord with Nehemiah's demands. But there is discord in this community, and it must have been painful for Nehemiah to face this reality. Also, most likely not everyone went along with the proposed restoration. Some may have said "amen" and "praise the Lord" (v. 13) and on second thought considered the whole enterprise too exorbitant. Or after initially making good on their promise, they may have returned to their former ways. So it may cost Nehemiah the goodwill and support of at least some of his natural allies.

A Well-Prepared Table (5:14–19)

For now, Nehemiah is interested more in clearing his name than in what he stands to lose. The last section of this chapter, verses 14–19, presents an elaborate self-defense on his part. Only now is it made clear that Nehemiah is the appointed governor over Judah. This fact is revealed in the context of a statement about his refusal to take from the community even the expenses that were his due, even though he has extensive costs and an elaborate court to feed and care for: "There were at my table one hundred fifty people, Jews and officials, besides those who came to us from the nations around us" (Neh. 5:17). The section ends with a prayer of self-recommendation: "Remember for my good, O my God, all that I have done for this people" (Neh. 5:10).

Is Nehemiah convincing? It may all sound a bit too good to be true. As the dangers may have been exaggerated in chapter 4, so here Nehemiah seems to aggrandize his virtues. Yet we keep his delicate position in mind. Nehemiah is not so much a hero as an all too human leader caught on the hook of conflicting loyalties.

A HOME RESTORED
Nehemiah 6 and 7

Plots Within and Without (6:1–14)

6:1 Now when it was reported to Sanballat and Tobiah and to Geshem the Arab and to the rest of our enemies that I had built the wall and that there was no gap left in it (though up to that time I had not set up the doors in the gates), ² Sanballat and Geshem sent to me, saying, "Come and let us meet together in one of the villages in the plain of Ono." But they intended to do me harm. ³ So I sent messengers to them, saying, "I am doing a great work and I cannot come down. Why should the work stop while I leave it to come down to you?"

Chapter 6 and the first verses of chapter 7 return to opposition to Nehemiah and Jerusalem from outside. This time, however, the enemy has found collaborators inside the community in Jerusalem. This collusion must have been particularly painful to Nehemiah and makes his life even more difficult, for it becomes harder to locate the opponents. The first section of chapter 6 describes an attempt by Sanballat to lure Nehemiah into a conference, to discredit him with the Persian court, and to entice him to sacrilege by entering the temple (Neh. 6:1–14). Nehemiah foils these efforts but in the process discovers at least one collaborator inside Jerusalem. This person was evidently not alone, for Nehemiah's prayer for retribution includes a group of prophets, to us unknown: "Remember Tobiah and Sanballat, O my God, according to these things that they did, and also the prophetess Noadiah and the rest of the prophets who wanted to make me afraid" (Neh. 6:14).

Even if the means of trapping Nehemiah seem so intricate and contrived as to appear ridiculous, the entire episode testifies to the very real threat to Nehemiah's leadership. The divisions inside, on the face of it healed by Nehemiah's ethical approach and stern measures as told in chapter 5, may well have left a group of malcontents in Judah ready to join hands with the outside opponents. The governorship of Nehemiah is experienced as a benefit by the less privileged classes, but the more well-to-do probably perceived him as a less obvious patron. Perhaps they felt that they did not need a governor like this. Such a model of integrity can be a thorn in the flesh of those who would rather make a quick profit, even if it causes further misery for others.

A Task Completed (6:15—7:4)

6:15 So the wall was finished on the twenty-fifth day of the month Elul, in fifty-two days. [16] And when all our enemies heard of it, all the nations around us were afraid and fell greatly in their own esteem; for they perceived that this work had been accomplished with the help of our God. [17] Moreover in those days the nobles of Judah sent many letters to Tobiah, and Tobiah's letters came to them. [18] For many in Judah were bound by oath to him, because he was the son-in-law of Shecaniah son of Arah: and his son Jehohanan had married the daughter of Meshullam son of Berechiah. [19] Also they spoke of his good deeds in my presence, and reported my words to him. And Tobiah sent letters to intimidate me.

The attempts of Sanballat and Tobiah described in this chapter are designed to frighten and discredit Nehemiah with the Persian power and his own community. To a degree, the persistent efforts of the enemies succeed. The wall is finished, so the record notes, in October 445. A remarkable accomplishment! Nehemiah and the community have brought their work to successful completion in a minimum of time, against the odds, and there is reason to celebrate. Yet Nehemiah's report sounds almost dispirited. The completion of the wall is occasion for further attempts to undermine his authority, with clear implications of folks inside Jerusalem involved in the matter. It now appears that Tobiah, one of the villains, is closely related to members of the community (Neh. 6:18). The "nobles of Judah" are making common cause with Tobiah and try to gain favor on his behalf with Nehemiah.

If it does not make sense that Tobiah at the same time tries to intimidate Nehemiah, we note that intrigues of this sort are seldom marked by logic. Their goal is to distress and destabilize Nehemiah, and it works to an extent. The wall is finished, the doors are set, but vigilance rather than celebration is the order of the day (Neh. 7:1–4). The gates stay closed much longer than would be usual, and guards are everywhere at their post on the lookout for trouble (Neh. 7:3). Finally, the last word about the rebuilt city highlights a lack of population and houses inside the city: "The city was wide and large, but the people within it were few and no houses had been built" (Neh. 7:4).

A Memorial of Names (7:5–73)

Chapter 7 offers another list of families, virtually identical to Ezra 2. The list serves to identify the first group of returned exiles and their descendants, and the motivation for unearthing it is to find appropriate inhabitants for Jerusalem. This list is more interesting for its placement and function in the Ezra-Nehemiah material than for the names it contains. The building projects of temple and city wall are now successfully brought to completion. Ezra 2 and Nehemiah 7 form a framework around the accounts of the work on the temple and wall construction. These projects took place in the context of a particular community, one that provided the impetus and the energy for the ongoing work. It is thus appropriate to recite the names of this community at the beginning and end of the work. Community and city complex stand in need of one another. One without the other functions only in part as a sign of God's presence.

In considering once again the function and importance of lists consisting of names in the Ezra-Nehemiah material, I was struck by an observation a friend made to me in a recent conversation. He told me that he views genealogical lists in Scripture in light of the AIDS quilt. The more than 70,000 names woven into the quilt give him a sense both of loss and restoration. Although there is great loss to be mourned, there is also a regeneration that has taken place in his community as it has come together to mourn *and* to celebrate the lives of AIDS victims. This profound insight may be useful to us as we contemplate the name lists in Ezra and Nehemiah.

Once, when I visited the Holocaust museum in Washington, D.C., I found myself in front of the partition on which are listed the names of the Gentiles who saved Jewish lives during the Second World War. These are called "the righteous Gentiles." I took note of the many names listed and for myself recited all the Dutch names I saw listed there. This project took quite some time, because there are many names in that particular list. As I stood there quietly reading familiar and unfamiliar names, I experienced some resolution to the painful process of coming to terms with my own past and the past of my people. In the United States, the Vietnam Memorial with its many names moves many people deeply, even if they have no intimate acquaintances listed on that wall. The community of the Restoration in Judah writes and recites the list of names in a process that is similar to the instances that I have provided here. The names themselves are in Hebrew and remain unfamiliar to us, but nothing is as far removed from our context as we might think.

In addition, in Nehemiah much attention is spent on the trials and troubles of the person of Nehemiah. The list brings the attention back to where it belongs, to the covenant community that is to live in the city. Ezra and Nehemiah are not so much about the central role of leaders as about the central place of the community in the ongoing life of the Jews. This community exists as yet in a fragmented and disunited fashion. Recorded divisions between wealthy and poor point to a very real social and religious distress in this period. In addition, the community is divided in its support for Nehemiah. Much still needs to be done to forge this group into a people who will have a strong identity as the people with whom God is in covenant.

The list thus functions also as a takeoff point for the chapters to follow, which describe the forging of a crowd into a people bound by common loyalty to the Torah, its directives and guidance, and thereby to God. Revived stones and a restored home are ready for a revived community.

4. Walking in God's Law
Nehemiah 8—10

These chapters concern themselves with a public recitation and interpretation of the Torah and the reactions to this reading on the part of the people. There is a shift in perspective relative to the previous material, where Nehemiah appears in a first person narrative. Here events are told in the third person, and Ezra reappears to take the lead in presenting the law to the community. First Ezra reads and his assistants explain the reading (Neh. 8:1–12). Then a number of reactions take place in the community in response to the understanding of the law. Celebration and repentance in turn mark the profound effect that the words of the Torah have on the people, who act in a united way to respond to the message (Neh. 8:13—9:37). Ezra recites a confessional prayer as lead-in to the signing of a pledge by the people and their representatives, a pledge that consists of a series of precise obligations (Neh. 9:38—10:39).

ATTENTIVE EARS
Nehemiah 8:1–12

At the Water Gate (8:1–8)

When the seventh month came—the people of Israel being settled in their towns—

8:1 all the people gathered together into the square before the Water Gate. They told the scribe Ezra to bring the book of the law of Moses, which the LORD had given to Israel. 2 Accordingly, the priest Ezra brought the law before the assembly, both men and women and all who could hear with understanding. This was on the first day of the seventh month. 3 He read from it facing the square before the Water Gate from early morning until midday, in the presence of the men and the women and those who could understand; and the ears of the people were attentive to the book of the law.

Whenever the people gather in the seventh month, there is an implicit understanding that worship and celebration are just around the corner, because this is one of the most important months in terms of the liturgical calendar of ancient Israel (see Ezra 3:1). There is no obvious reason for the people to come together; the text does not present this gathering as a result of a call by Ezra or anyone else. Rather, the meeting takes place, and then Ezra is told to bring the book of the law. In the way the text poses it, the initiative for both meeting and reading of the law lies with the people rather than the leaders. The assigning of initiative to the assembly is significant, for this is the very crowd in which divisions and injustice have divided neighbor from neighbor, according to the previous narrative. It is as if the fractured community goes in search of its own healing.

The role of the people stays central throughout this section and the one following. They are the subject of the meeting; they request the reading of the law and make it possible for Ezra to hold a public reading on a platform "made for the purpose" (Neh. 8:4). The centrality of the community to the proceedings is underlined by the repetition of the word "people" or the phrase "all the people" (vv. 1, 5, 6, 7, 8, 9, 11, 12), sometimes varied by "the men and the women and those who could understand" (vv. 2, 3) and a list of names of assistants (vv. 4, 7). In fact, only verse 10 lacks an explicit reference of this kind.

Ezra comes back into the picture because his guidance is significant in relation to the law rather than to building programs. Also, Ezra's position is not potentially compromised by being in the pay of the empire, unlike governor Nehemiah. Whether Ezra and Nehemiah were active at the same time is not so much a significant issue to the writer of this material. It is more important that their activities were complementary. Thus Ezra continues where Nehemiah left off. The people who will find a home in the repaired city and who worship in the restored temple are clearly in need of guidance. Guidance and direction are provided by the "book of the law of Moses" (Neh. 8:1) through the agency of the scribe Ezra.

We may understand the reference to the book of the law as the first five books of the Bible, Genesis through Deuteronomy, in more or less the same form as they exist today. Moses was for a long time understood to be the author of these texts. As noted already, "law" is a term that covers only in part what the books contain. When Ezra stands up to read, he reads about the creation of the world and of Israel as a people; he reads about the failings of humanity and of the covenant community; he reads all the ups and downs of the history of God with the world and with God's people until they reach the land of the promise. He reads stories and poems, songs and blessings, and also "laws." The people who listen to Ezra listen to a recital of the past and of the way God went with them in the past. One of the decisive moments in this history came when the people were shaped into a community by entering into a covenant with their God.

The story as it is told in Exodus 19—24 tells of the gathering of the slaves who had escaped Egypt under the leadership of Moses and Aaron and Miriam. Moses was for the people also the go-between in terms of their relationship with God. Moses it was who received the set of laws that formed the core of the prescriptions God laid out for the people (Exod. 20:1–17). Moses presided over the rites by which God and the people were bound into a covenant. (Exod. 24:3–8). When the people were at that time pledged as covenant partners with God, they promised to *do* the words God gave them and to *listen* to God's voice (Exod. 24:7). This covenant made at Mount Sinai provided for the slaves who escaped from Egypt a means by which they were forged into something other than a crowd. These folk became a community in covenant with God. In order to live their common life in agreement with this covenant they received guidance, direction, or instruction—in Hebrew, *torah*. *Torah* means also "law," but is essentially a great deal more than material we would view as law or rules. *Torah* includes stories and poems and long lists of names, all the material that serves to instruct the people as to where they have come from, who they are, and how they should live. Ancient Israel viewed this instruction as coming directly from God, via human agency. The five books, Genesis through Deuteronomy, are together named after this divine instruction, the Torah.

Although some of the material may have been written down from the time of its conception, essentially *torah* was not a book. Gradually the materials that constituted *torah* were written down and gathered into collections until they became what now constitutes the first five books of the Bible. This process, we think, was for the most part completed by the time Ezra and Nehemiah were doing their work. The change from ongoing dynamic process of *torah* into a written document constitutes the first formation of sacred text, or Bible, as we know it.

The people who listen to Ezra listen not only to a story of the past, but they listen to how this story and these instructions might guide them at this moment. The situation is not identical to the time of the exodus, but there are similarities. There is the fact that in essence these folk too are the ones who have come from captivity. Especially, there is similarity in the need for a new community to form itself under the guidance that God provides for them. Unlike the situation at the time of the exodus, when Moses was the only one to mediate between God and people, here Ezra is surrounded by assistants. Both lay folk and Levites, by their presence at Ezra's side, betoken the presence of the people. Later, the Levites fill the role of interpreters (Neh. 8:7). Also, practically speaking, Ezra may have needed help, for he was reading from a scroll, rather than a book, and the scroll probably had to be held and unrolled by others.

It is, in any case, clear from this event that the book of the Torah of Moses given to Israel by the Lord is seen as central to the life of the community. This idea may be strange to a church that believes itself to be freed from the need of the law and that views obedience to the law as legalism to be avoided. It is helpful then to remember two things: *torah* is more than law; it is also the story that identifies the roots of the community especially in its relation to God, and it helps the community to give shape to its current self-understanding. The story of the past gives guidance for present and future. Second, insofar as the laws are a part of *torah*, they are an essential ingredient for a community that seeks guidance. At the time of Ezra-Nehemiah, the community listens to rules and prescriptions for its common life, and it does this in a way that seeks to apply these rules to a different time than when the laws were first constructed. Laws in ancient Israel went through long processes of adaptation and change. Rigidity and a static understanding of *torah* are not helpful. We keep in mind, however, that a rigid and literal understanding of the laws is more likely to occur when these laws are collected in a document than when their collection and formation is still fluid.

Basically, the community is listening for the voice of God, as did the community of their ancestors when they made their first covenant with God. Therefore the community of Ezra-Nehemiah is said to have "attentive ears" (8:3). This assembly in the late fifth century B.C.E. will not live perfectly in accordance with the guidance that they learn at this moment. The model for us today does not lie in the perfection with which predecessors followed the direction they received in their time. Rather, it may be beneficial for us as Christians to consider how *torah* can help us in our time. *Torah* is designed to help in figuring out where we came from, how God went with us in our history, and what the principles are on which we should formulate the regulations for the conduct of our common life. Like the Jews of Ezra's day, we may need to learn about the principle of justice that undergirds the covenant life, justice that expresses itself first and most of all in the care we extend to the disadvantaged.

Verses 4–8 of this chapter provide a vivid picture of the process that Ezra and his assistants follow in the reading, as well as the people's responses. Ezra reads from a platform while the assistants hold the scroll and unroll it. Later, the Levites explain the reading. Three times the text reiterates that there was explanation or interpretation going on while the text was read: "the Levites helped the people to understand the law" (Neh. 8:7). "So they read from the book, from the law of God, with interpretation. They gave the sense, so that the people understood the reading" (Neh. 8:8). At the end of the episode, the declaration sounds once more: "because they had understood the words that were declared to them" (Neh. 8:12). "With interpretation" may mean the translation of the words from Hebrew into Aramaic, the language of the people at the time. But we may assume also that there was interpretation in the sense of explanation, especially for texts that were difficult to understand. From having *attentive ears* the people can thus proceed to *understanding*.

A Holy Day (8:9–12)

From what follows we learn that the reaction of the people took the form of grieving: "For all the people wept when they heard the words of the law" (v. 9). Three times they are admonished not to do so by the leaders and teachers. Each person or group is identified by the role they play in the life of the community: "Nehemiah, who was the governor, and Ezra the priest and scribe, and the Levites who taught the people" (Neh. 8:9). These tell the people not to "mourn or weep" (v. 9) and not to be "grieved" (vv. 10 and 11). It should not surprise us too much that Nehemiah and Ezra are here mentioned as if their work and lives overlapped. The important fact for the writer of these events is not to convey exact historical data but the realities that he or she views as most significant for the period. The leadership of Nehemiah and Ezra in relation to their individual contributions has already been reviewed in the story. Nehemiah supports the restoration of the community through building programs and reforms of the social structures; Ezra is the one who restores the community through a focus on the Torah. Here the two are shown together as having an active role in interpreting the Torah for the community. The activity that centers on the Torah brings especially Nehemiah into the teaching and interpreting function. Without this function, in which Nehemiah *and* Ezra address the vitality of the community and its potential to regain an identity even under foreign domination, the leadership of Nehemiah might have lacked the necessary underpinning.

Why are the people distressed? Two verbs, *mourn* and *weep*, indicate actions that accompanied loss or any kind of national or individual disaster in ancient Israel. Fasting, tearing of hair and clothes, putting dust on one's head, sitting on the ground would be typical accompanying practices. (See also Ezra 9:3 and Job 2:13.) We may imagine that some of these actions, at least, are taking place at the Water Gate in Jerusalem at the time of the reading of the Torah, even though they are not mentioned explicitly. Weeping was most likely more a loud lamenting than a quiet shedding of tears, especially under these circumstances. The verb *grieve* occurs twice in verses 9–12 (vv. 10, 11). The Hebrew word so translated is not very common in the Bible but occurs elsewhere when the reaction of a person is a mixture of guilt and sadness when caught in a conflict of personal loyalty. So Jonathan is potentially *grieved* because of David in a situation that has him trapped between the conflicting loyalties toward his father and his friend, causing guilt toward the one and sadness toward the other (1 Sam. 20:3); Joseph admonishes his brothers not to be *grieved* that they had sold him, an occasion that was steeped in a mixture of conflicting loyalties (Gen. 45:5); and David, after the death of his traitor son, Absalom, is said to *mourn, weep,* and *grieve,* with the same sequence of the verbs as those used in Nehemiah 8:9–11. The attitude and behavior of David toward this son had been filled with conflicted loyalty, torn as he was between his fatherhood and his kingship, and his grief at this point was probably also permeated with guilt.

The community in Jerusalem in the days of Ezra and Nehemiah has listened to the stories and songs and laws of its origins. It is faced with a sense of loss and shame, for the land of the promise is no longer theirs in truth. Great sadness causes them to *mourn* and *weep.* Moreover, they believe this loss to have been because of their faithlessness. Some of the harsher speeches of Deuteronomy would have especially underlined this conviction. And so they *grieve* when they hear words such as these: "The LORD will bring you, and the king whom you set over you, to a nation that neither you nor your ancestors have known, where you shall serve other gods, of wood and stone" (Deut. 28:36). Or: "The LORD will bring a nation from far away, from the end of the earth, to swoop down on you like an eagle, a nation whose language you do not understand" (Deut. 28:49). And: "Although once you were as numerous as the stars in heaven, you shall be left few in number, because you did not obey the LORD your God" (Deut. 28:62). These things had indeed happened to them, and they believe they know why they had happened. So a profound sadness and guilt are the first reaction to their understanding of what is read to them.

But their instructors admonish them to change their reactions. They must rather engage in celebration appropriate to the festival time indicated by the seventh month; eat and drink and share provisions with the poor. Those actions too were prescribed in Deuteronomy (Deut. 14:29 and 26:12–13). The people have heard and understood, but even with understanding one may hear all too selectively. This is a time, so the leaders say, to rejoice, for the people's strength is located in their joy rather than in their grief. Three times the motivation for abstaining from tears is provided with the statement that this is a holy day. The word "holy" in the Bible is complex. We may remember that it means "set aside," or "separate." When holy is used as an adjective for God, it points indeed to God's otherness. But also and perhaps paradoxically, the holiness of God indicates God's dedication to the creation and to God's people. (See Hos. 11:9, for example). The people who make up God's covenant community are not by nature holy, but they are called to be holy. "You shall be holy, for I the LORD your God am holy" (Lev. 19:2). This means that they are called to dedicate themselves to a life in which they emulate God's dedication to the welfare of humanity, with embedded in it God's special passionate concern for the downtrodden.

To declare a day "holy to the Lord," means for the community to set it aside, to dedicate it to God in joyful remembering of who they are and who God is. Such remembering is typically accompanied by acts of kindness and generosity toward those who are less well endowed with provisions, who have no abundance to share. God is, after all is said and done, abundant in goodness toward the people. God has rescued them once more from captivity; their holy place, symbolized by temple and city, is rebuilt. Surely joy rather than sadness is called for. Also, God's abundant goodness needs to find concrete expression in human actions from neighbor to neighbor. And so the section ends with a mention of these activities. Instead of mourning, weeping, and grieving, there is eating and drinking, sharing of food and gladness. First must come celebration; there will be time later for confession and repentance.

We might think this a turning upside down of the appropriate order. In our liturgy, confession comes before celebration. This is apparently also how the community in Jerusalem considered it. What takes place here by order of the leaders is a reversal of the ordinary way of doing things. Sometimes individuals or groups may be so beaten down already that the first thing they need is to regain a sense of happiness over their survival. They may need to be reminded first of their strength and resources rather than of their sins. Only after they have done so can a remembrance of past and present trespasses take place.

FEASTS AND FASTS
Nehemiah 8:13—9:37

A Festival Restored (8:13–18)

8:13 On the second day the heads of ancestral houses of all the people, with the priests and the Levites, came together to the scribe Ezra in order to study the words of the law. ¹⁴ And they found it written in the law, which the LORD had commanded by Moses, that the people of Israel should live in booths during the festival of the seventh month. . . . ¹⁷ And all the assembly of those who had returned from the captivity made booths and lived in them; for from the days of Jeshua son of Nun to that day the people of Israel had not done so. And there was very great rejoicing. ¹⁸ And day by day, from the first day to the last day, he read from the book of the law of God. They kept the festival seven days; and on the eighth day there was a solemn assembly, according to the ordinance.

Celebration continues, instigated this time by representatives of the people, the family heads and temple personnel who together with Ezra engage in further study of the Torah. They find prescribed in it for this very month the exact manner in which to celebrate the festival that recalled the people's wandering through the wilderness after the exodus from Egypt before they reached the promised land. The festival of booths or tabernacles, in Hebrew *Sukkot*, was one of the three main festivals of the ancient Israelite community. It commemorated the marvelous escape of the slaves from Egypt and their journey through the wilderness under God's protection. It was a joy-filled feast of thanksgiving held at the time of the autumnal harvest. The prescriptions for it can be found in Exodus, Leviticus, and Deuteronomy (Exod. 23:16; 34:22; Lev. 23:23–44; Deut. 16:13–15).

The structure we need to envision with the word *booth* is that of a simple, temporary hut or shelter constructed of branches. The original connection of this festival was with agriculture rather than the people's history. In Palestine and elsewhere, temporary structures are still erected at harvest time. These "booths" perform a multiple function. They are a gathering place to deposit and sort the fruit; they provide shelter against the elements when necessary; and they can be the center for the workers to gather and have refreshment or a pause in their labor. In the countryside of my youth such stalls marked the time and place of fruit harvest from May through September. They were set up in the orchards and functioned also as market stalls from which the fruit could be sold to passersby. Harvest time has been a period for celebration from days immemorial. In the Exodus and Deuteronomic account of the feast of booths the agricultural nature of this festival is still clear. Gradually, the community transformed this occasion into one that commemorated the sacred story of the people's travels in the wilderness. The booths were then indicative of the temporary quality of the community's dwelling in the desert before they arrived in Canaan and at the same time of God's guidance and presence with them in that period. The Leviticus text speaks of God making "the people of Israel live in booths when I brought them out of the land of Egypt" (Lev. 23:43). This is a symbolic rather than a literal truth, for the people did not trek through the wilderness in such booths, but rather in tents.

The text of Nehemiah 8:13–18 describes in detail how the festival is celebrated (vv. 15–16) to underline the faithfulness with which Torah is followed. The entire celebration stresses the fact that the people's celebration is like that of the escaped slaves from Egypt. Here too are found "those who had returned from the captivity" (v. 17). As in the wilderness long ago, in current circumstances too the people may count on God's protection and celebrate God's kindness. Against all the odds, they are in the process of becoming a restored community. Their once ruined temple and broken-down city are once more standing, a place for them to dwell in; their numbers may be reduced, but they have survived. Their status may be no higher than those of the band of slaves that trekked through the wilderness centuries before them, but they have put themselves under God's aegis, as their ancestors had done, even if the more immediate power over them is that of the king of Persia.

The entire restored city becomes the place for this celebration: the houses, the courts, and the squares (v. 16). The "house of God" is mentioned as one place among many for the placing of the festival booths. We may have expected the temple to be more in the center of such a holy day, but here it almost blends in with its surroundings of city dwellings and streets. Apart from the fact that the idea of the holy place is not confined to the temple alone but embraces the entire city, there is more at stake here. The feast of booths in its final, transformed understanding reminds the community also of a time before there was a temple. That was a time when the people were on the move and God moved with them "in a tent and a tabernacle" (2 Sam. 7:6). To that time the community looks for its origins and for the early promises of God's presence with them. In the end, that presence does not depend on any place or structure but resides in God's loyalty to them, freely given. Structures, even those made of the sturdiest materials, may in the end turn out as temporary as booths made of branches. The people's hope rests rather in the permanent promise of God's covenant with them. Understood in this way, temporary shelter evokes permanent presence.

In addition, the words of the Torah, "as it was written," dominate the action of these sections. The scroll is in the center, and the identity of the community reshapes itself around the scroll. As divided as they had become according to earlier descriptions, so are they now unified in their reactions to the Torah. *All the people* wept, *all the assembly* made booths, and *the people of Israel* repented (see chap. 9).

The text states that there had not been a celebration like this since the days of Joshua. It would be hard to believe that such a central festival could at any time have been forgotten in the liturgical calendar of the community. Also, the biblical text testifies to its being held at several points in ancient Israel's history. (See Judg. 21:19; 1 Sam. 1:3; and Ezra 3:4, for example.) What is intended here is perhaps the manner in which all the people can be gathered into one location, Jerusalem. There is an advantage in small numbers, after all. Or, a very human tendency to highlight and exaggerate comes here to the fore: "I tell you, you haven't seen anything like it ever! No, not for hundreds of years!"

A Fast and a Prayer (9:1–37)

9:32 "Now, therefore, our God—the great and mighty and awesome God, keeping covenant and steadfast love—do not treat lightly all the hardship that has come upon us, upon our kings, our officials, our priests, our prophets, our ancestors, and all your people, since the time of the kings of Assyria until today. 33 You have been just in all that has come upon us, for you have dealt faithfully and we have acted wickedly; 34 our kings, our officials, our priests, and our ancestors have not kept your law or heeded the commandments and the warnings that you gave them. 35 Even in their own kingdom, and in the great goodness you bestowed on them, and in the large and rich land that you set before them, they did not serve you and did not turn from their wicked works. 36 Here we are, slaves to this day—slaves in the land that you gave to our ancestors to enjoy its fruit and its good gifts. 37 Its rich yield goes to the kings whom you have set over us because of our sins; they have power also over our bodies and over our livestock at their pleasure, and we are in great distress."

Now the moment has arrived for repentance and confession. Once more the people gather, this time engaged in symbolic actions of repentance. They fast, put on sackcloth, and pour earth on their heads (Neh. 9:1).

Evidently, the earlier grieving had been premature, and now the leaders do nothing to discourage the community from expressing their sadness and shame over their failures. Their previous celebration and expressions of joy form the foundation on which confession can be made. In verses 1–5, community and leaders join in confession and reading of the Torah. In their confessing, the people separate themselves from "all foreigners" (v. 2) to emphasize their identity as descendants of Israel, that is to say, in this case those who are in need of confession.

This is the third reading of the Torah mentioned in these chapters, emphasizing that everything that happens in these episodes is centered on the Torah. As previously, the reading causes a response, this time in the form of a long prayer that consists of a rehearsal of God's goodness toward Israel in the past and of the people's faithlessness in return. It is almost more a sermon than a prayer. Also, the language is hardly original, and for almost every verse a parallel can be found elsewhere in Scripture. Such prayers may not speak to our imagination or interest, and we may be impatient with sermons that dress up as prayer. In addition, penitential prayer may not be a strong point in our Christian liturgies. After short and formalized prayers of confession, we move quickly to more important issues. Certainly, an entire penitential service as we find it here is not familiar to us. There may be something to learn about the importance of such a focus at appropriate times.

After the introductory phrases (v. 6), which set everything that follows in the context of God's concern with the entire creation, the prayer offers a review of the way God has gone with the people Israel. The history of God with the people is divided into three episodes: the covenant with Abraham (vv. 7–8); the exodus from Egypt and journey through the wilderness (vv. 9–22); and the possession and loss of the land of the promise (vv. 23–31). The longest section is that devoted to the exodus and stay in the wilderness, with specific references to the giving of *torah* at Sinai (vv. 13–14). Implicitly, a strong connection is drawn between the assembly in Jerusalem of the fifth century B.C.E. and the slaves whom God liberated from Egypt.

The intent of the prayer is first to recite God's goodness. God's gracious actions toward Israel therefore receive the most attention. The God who is the creator of all that is, is also the God who made a covenant with Abram, who delivered the slaves from Egypt, guided them in the wilderness with *torah* and bread, and established them in the land of the promise (Neh. 9:1–25). At the heart of this praise stands verse 17b: "But you are a God ready to forgive, gracious and merciful, slow to anger and abounding in steadfast love, and you did not forsake them." Such a recitation of God's gracious nature can be found elsewhere in the Bible with some variations. (See, for example, Exod. 34:6; Num. 14:18; Pss. 86:15; 103:8; Joel 2:13; Jon. 4:2.) Here the phrase "and you did not forsake them" is added, and is repeated at the end of the rehearsal in verse 31: "Nevertheless, in your great mercies you did not make an end of them or forsake them, for you are a gracious and merciful God."

Second, the prayer highlights Israel's rebellious and disobedient behavior toward God. The recital of Israel's faithlessness is cast in stereotypical general language: "They acted presumptuously . . . they stiffened their necks . . . they did not obey" are the most frequently repeated phrases in reference to sin in verses 16–31 (vv.16, 26, 29). Arrogance, stubbornness, and disobedience were the cause of the disaster that befell Israel: "Therefore you handed them over to the peoples of the lands" (v. 30). Yet the overview ends with the statement about God's mercy cited above (v. 31). All of the prayer until this point is in the third person. This is the story of God's presence with the *ancestors* and the rebellious reaction of these ancestors toward God's goodness. In the end, however, the prayer allows little distance between the ancestors and the community of Ezra-Nehemiah's time. With the switch to the first person plural in verse 32, the sins of the ancestors become "our" sins. Verses 33 and 34 make abundantly clear what is at the heart of the issue: "you have dealt faithfully and we have acted wickedly" (v. 33).

In verse 32 the tone of the prayer changes from recital of the past, with an emphasis on God's goodness and Israel's disobedience, to a plea for God to be merciful once more. God is again reminded of God's power and loyalty and is implored not to trivialize the present trouble. The last lines of the prayer depict graphically the reality of the situation for the Jerusalem community, dominated as it is by foreign rule, even if the city is restored and the temple rebuilt. They no longer "possess" this land, but are slaves in it on whom the demands of the empire weigh heavily.

Penitential prayers of this type, including a review of Israel's history and God's merciful deeds in the past, can be found in the psalms. (See Pss. 78, 105, 106, for example.) Such psalms may open and close with an expression of praise to God; they do not ordinarily end with a description of current anguish. In Nehemiah 9 the usual progression is reversed; praise opens the prayer and a sharply focused description of misery closes it. The community is not let off the hook anywhere in the course of the prayer. The community in past and present has sinned. Because God is faithful and merciful even in the midst of much provocation, God may be asked to be merciful once again and pay attention to the people in their woeful situation.

In the English translation, the final word of the prayer is *distress*. In Hebrew the final word is *we*. Literally, the text reads at the end of verse 37: "in great distress are we." The prayer opens, both in English and Hebrew, with the word "You," referring to God. These pronouns, *you* and *we*, stand as brackets around the entire prayer, the first directing the attention to God, the second putting the focus on the community. This entire business is after all a matter between God and the community, between *you* and *us*. As slaves the people are oriented toward the foreign king who rules them because of their sins. As the people of God's covenant love, they are ultimately responsible to God and God is responsible for them. Precisely as an anguished community, the assembly reorients itself to its true ruler, guide, and protector.

The history of the people began in oppression in Egypt (v. 9). From this situation God delivered them. After a long history of ups and downs, of gain and loss, the final note is one of distress. Although at the moment returned to the land of the promises, these escapees faced continued hardship under foreign domination. Verses 36 and 37 draw attention to the present community and its situation by framing the lines in the phrases with a first person plural: "Here we are . . . We are in great distress."

A WRITTEN PLEDGE
Nehemiah 9:38—10:39

Torah Implementation (9:38—10:27)

9:38 Because of all this we make a firm agreement in writing, and on that sealed document are inscribed the names of our officials, our Levites, and our priests.
10:1 Upon the sealed document are the names of Nehemiah the governor, son of Hacaliah, and Zedekiah; [2] Seraiah, Azariah, Jeremiah, [3] Pashhur, Amariah, Malchijah, [4] Hattush, Shebaniah, Malluch, [5] Harim, Meremoth, Obadiah, [6] Daniel, Ginnethon, Baruch, [7] Meshullam, Abijah, Mijamin, [8] Maaziah, Bilgai, Shemaiah; these are the priests. [9] And the Levites: Jeshua son of Azaniah, Binnui of the sons of Henadad, Kadmiel; [10] and their associates, Shebaniah, Hodiah, Kelita, Pelaiah, Hanan, [11] Mica, Rehob, Hashabiah, [12] Zaccur, Sherebiah, Shebaniah, [13] Hodiah, Bani, Beninu. [14] The leaders of the people: Parosh, Pahath-moab, Elam, Zattu, Bani, [15] Bunni, Azgad, Bebai, [16] Adonijah, Bigvai, Adin, [17] Ater, Hezekiah, Azzur, [18] Hodiah, Hashum, Bezai, [19] Hariph, Anathoth, Nebai, [20] Magpiash, Meshullam, Nezir, [21] Meshezabel, Zadok, Jaddua, [22] Pelatiah, Hanan, Anaiah, [23] Hoshea, Hana-

niah, Hasshub, [24] Hallohesh, Pilha, Shobek, [25] Rehum, Hashabnah, Maaseiah, [26] Ahiah, Hanan, Anan, [27] Malluch, Harim, and Baanah.

In line with the importance of the lists of names in this material and to honor their significance not only for the past but also for today, I have included this one list in full. I invite us to recite the names as best we can. These names were meant to be recited aloud and are collected in series of threes to enable easier and more rhythmic recital. Only in verses 10 and 14 is the regularity broken by the presentation of five names. Not only the leaders, the priests and the Levites, are named here, but also the lay folk. Some names that occur are duplicated in other lists; others are different. The entire community is in the picture at this moment that concludes the series of responses to the Torah. There has been grief, joyous celebration, and confession. The time has arrived for the renewed community to make new commitments.

Walking in God's Law (10:28–39)

10:28 **The rest of the people, the priests, the Levites, the gatekeepers, the singers, the temple servants, and all who have separated themselves from the peoples of the lands to adhere to the law of God, their wives, their sons, their daughters, all who have knowledge and understanding, [29] join with their kin, their nobles, and enter into a curse and an oath to walk in God's law, which was given by Moses the servant of God, and to observe and do all the commandments of the LORD our Lord and his ordinances and his statutes.**

As were all the previous reactions, the pledges now taken and preserved in a sealed document are inspired by the Torah, and they form the last implementation of the Torah recorded in this material. The central role of the Torah in the formation of the community could not be stated more clearly. The agreements that are made relate to the life of the people in its social and religious dimensions and are eminently practical. They are of interest to us not so much because of their particulars as for the evidence of the strong linkage between the religious and the social life. Both of these aspects of life are inspired by Torah; both are in need of divine guidance.

The particular agreements give evidence of reading the Torah in light of the times and their predicaments. In verses 30–39 of this chapter three issues are addressed: (1) relations to outsiders in terms of family; (2) relations to outsiders and neighbors in holy times; and (3) relations to the temple and its personnel. Each concern speaks directly to the self-identification of the community.

1. Verse 30: Intermarriage with "the peoples of the land" is viewed as detrimental to the identity of the faith community, just as we encountered it in Ezra 9—10. Yet we notice that the hostility, as well as the anxiety, that was apparent in some of the Ezra material is here lacking and that no retroactive measures are taken. We may still have difficulty with such a strict attitude. In many of our own communities of faith, however, marrying outside of one's denomination, letting go one's faith community, may still be seen as highly problematic. Furthermore, the issue for this small community is literally one of survival in extremely difficult times. The attitude and practice is not so much one to admire and emulate as it is one to recognize and understand as common to human communities across the centuries.

The commerce that is not permitted in verse 31 is specifically with "the peoples of the land." It is perhaps not so much the buying of food itself that is renounced, but in particular, buying from those outside the community. Continuing the concern stated in verse 30, verse 31 speaks also to the need to define oneself *over against* others, to separate oneself from other groups. This need became greater as the small province of Judah became more and more engulfed by large empires and as the pressure for the Jews to assimilate to the reigning culture became stronger.

2. Verse 31: "and if the peoples of the land bring in merchandise or any grain on the sabbath day to sell, we will not buy it from them on the sabbath or on a holy day; and we will forego the crops of the seventh year and the exaction of every debt." This prohibition concerns itself with associations and practices on the sabbath or other festival days and in the seventh year. The sabbath was traditionally in ancient Israel a day set aside for rest and cessation of labor. (See Exod. 20:8–10; 34:21; Deut. 5:12–15.) The Torah does not forbid commerce explicitly in any of the laws pertaining to the sabbath, although it is easy to understand trade as implicitly included in labor. For the Jewish community in exile, the sabbath took on an even greater significance than it had before the destruction of city and temple. To keep *Shabbat* in exile was one of the identifying marks that set the Jews apart from their context in Babylon. It was also a custom that could be kept everywhere, because it did not depend on a special place or structure. The sabbath afforded, moreover, an opportunity for celebrating the communion with God and neighbor in prayer and by reading sacred texts. Out of such occasions the earliest synagogues may have arisen. Synagogue literally means "gathering," and its practices may well date as far back as the early exilic period in the first half of the sixth century B.C.E.

In the Protestant community of my upbringing in Holland, sabbath was kept quite rigorously on Sundays. In our household, not a strict one by any standards then or today, everyone took time off from work. Neither of my parents had any dealings that involved money except for what they gave to the offering during the worship service. My own rules included finishing my homework on Saturday so I would be free of it on Sundays. Temptations to spend money were limited in our theater-less town where the shops closed on Sundays. Certain dilemmas did not present themselves to me until later. I well remember with what difficulty I made a decision in my early twenties to see a film on Ascension Day!

Such rules may seem trivial and alien to us today, where neither culture nor faith community may do much to distinguish Sunday from other days beyond the attending of a worship service. Sabbath may never make a comeback. What I valued as a youngster was the time off, the sense of "holy" time that Sunday provided, and the definite rhythm of the week established by this seventh day of rest. For the postexilic Jewish community, all of these aspects were probably important, but above all the sabbath observance became bound up with who they were as a faith community. At this period the community in Judah is in the process of procuring for itself the means of its survival beyond the loss of land and temple by investing its sense of itself in sacred time and text as well as in sacred space.

The second half of verse 31 combines two laws in an imaginative way. A law that prescribed letting the soil lie fallow on the seventh year is to the immediate detriment of those who farm it; exempting debt is to the immediate disadvantage of those who charged it. By combining these laws, the parties ideally come out even. (See Exod. 23:10–11 and Deut. 15:1–8.) Through interpreting and applying the laws in a creative and flexible way, new possibilities arise for all. Even if these rules do not create automatic equity, the desire for greater equity among the different classes is apparent.

3. Verses 32–39: The third agreement regulates the relations of the community to its sacred place, the temple. The last set of the three agreements taken on by the pledge-takers, and the most elaborate one, is the pledge for the upkeep of "the house of our God." This term is repeated eight times in the span of eight verses (Neh. 10:32–39). The final phrase encapsulates the intention of the entire section: "We will not neglect the house of our God (v. 39). The usage of "the house of our God" stands out both because of its frequency in this passage and because it is rare in the Bible elsewhere (Ps. 135:2 and Joel 1:16). The only other reference to the temple in these chapters occurs in 8:16, where the temple is one place among many for the construction of booths. The centrality of the concern with the temple is brought back by the repeated mention in chapter 8, and at the same time this mention functions as a link with the following chapters where the holy place will once more be at the center of attention.

Detailed obligations for the regular upkeep of offerings and service in the temple and for the maintenance of temple personnel are provided in this section. In most of the verses the people are in charge of the action, with the word "people" that predominated in the first part of the eighth chapter here replaced by "we": "We also lay on ourselves the obligation to charge ourselves . . . for the rows of bread. . . . We have also cast lots. . . . We obligate ourselves to bring . . . also to bring . . . and to bring. . . . We will not neglect. . . . " This repeated use of the first person plural leaves little doubt as to where the initiative, as well as the execution of the obligations, rests. Rather than the leadership coming to the fore with these actions, *the people* commit themselves to be actively involved in the temple's continued function. The community that went in search of its healing has found the guidance it sought in the Torah. The people have mourned in response, they have celebrated, they have confessed—three responses that were dictated in the main by the past and the present. In making new commitments, the community directs itself to the future.

5. Reclaiming the House
Nehemiah 11—13

These concluding chapters tie up the loose ends remaining in the narrative. After the account of the successful restoration of the city walls, an announcement was made of the scarcity of inhabitants for the city (Neh. 7:4). The first item of business here concerns itself with repopulating Jerusalem (Nehemiah 11). A list of names is appended of those who come from outside to live in Jerusalem. Because city and temple are closely related, a list of persons who serve the temple is added (Neh. 12:1–25). The restoration of both structures and community makes appropriate celebrations possible, and the city walls are dedicated (Neh. 12:27–47). The last chapter is concerned with implementation of the agreements concluded in chapter 10. Nehemiah is once more in the foreground in this last section, and in this manner his presence brackets all of the Nehemiah material (Nehemiah 13).

INHABITING THE HOUSE
Nehemiah 11:1—12:26

A Tithe of People (11:1–2)

11:1 **Now the leaders of the people lived in Jerusalem; and the rest of the people cast lots to bring one out of ten to live in the holy city Jerusalem, while nine-tenths remained in the other towns.** 2 **And the people blessed all those who willingly offered to live in Jerusalem.**

These sentences are constructed around a few central notions. The first one, Jerusalem, occurs three times, with the addition "the holy city" in verse 1. This addition underlines the understanding of the city as a holy place, and the notion of the city as an extension of the temple is thereby highlighted. The terminology "holy city" to indicate Jerusalem is relatively rare in the Bible. It occurs again in this chapter of Nehemiah in verse

18. By extending the notion of holiness to the entire city, the first lines of chapter 11 connect with the last words of the preceding chapter, "the house of our God." The promise made there not to "neglect" the house of God finds also a resolution in repopulating the city.

"People" and "live" are two other words that are central to these verses. This passage continues the emphasis on the people, the community that has set its footsteps on the path of *torah*, at this point connecting this focus with the concern about the place, Jerusalem, the holy city. City and temple restored, the community having gained a renewed sense of its identity, there yet remain problems. A place without inhabitants is not much of a place, after all. As in the events immediately preceding this account, the people are in the foreground. *They* cast lots to decide who will live in the empty house, and *they* bless those who are willing to move. In an echo of the tithing of produce in behalf of the temple in verse 38 of chapter 10, here a tithing of human beings takes place. One tenth of them will live in Jerusalem, a number important for its symbolic power. The temple will receive its tithes; the city also will receive tithes in the form of inhabitants.

To cast lots may strike us as a frivolous enterprise. Chance rather than God seems to be in charge here. The casting of lots in scripture, however, always sets up echoes of divine rather than human involvement. (See, for example, Josh. 14:2; Jon. 1:7.) Also, there is precedent in scripture for assigning dwelling places by means of casting lots. In the book of Joshua the lot had decided the apportionment of the promised land. One may safely assume here that those on whom the lot falls are understood to be appointed by God to move into Jerusalem. With a fine touch of irony, the ones chosen by lot are named volunteers. Note also that, unlike the situation in Joshua, the people themselves rather than the leaders cast the lots, in proper continuation of the primary place occupied by the community in these chapters.

Why, we may ask, would anyone hesitate to move into Jerusalem? Our imagination may provide possible answers to that question. Some folks who lived in the country may have been used to rural or small-town life, and the thought of living in a city may not have appealed to them at all. Even though cities at the time of Ezra-Nehemiah were very small compared to our understanding of what constitutes a city, many people may have viewed Jerusalem as a metropolis buzzing with all the problems we associate with cities today: poverty, violence, and loss of community. Also, and perhaps most of all, Jerusalem had proven itself to be a fragile, vulnerable place. On it the brunt of hostile attacks had fallen generations ago. It was Jerusalem that had been devastated and Jerusalem's population that had been deported. This "holy city" had been the primary target of the conquering armies of

Babylon during the first decades of the sixth century B.C.E. Jerusalem must have felt to many like a haunted place, a ghost town, where the memories of war's devastation lingered longest. Who wants to live in a place like that?

Population of the Holy City (11:3—12:26)

Yet this Jerusalem is precisely *the holy city*, the place that symbolizes for the Jewish community the presence of God and their own dedication to this God. In such a city all the inhabitants need to be legitimated by their ancestry. The list of names in 11:3–18 contains lay leaders with their genealogies, the names of the ancestors and a line of descent. The second time the term "holy city" occurs in the passage it concludes the genealogical part of the list; Jerusalem understood as holy city thus surrounds the inhabitants together with their ancestral lines (Neh. 11:18). More names follow as well as a listing of geographical locations outside of Jerusalem, almost certainly a listing of the ideal rather than the actual areas. (Neh. 11:25–36). Lists form links between past and present, and in Nehemiah 11—12 they link lay folk with temple personnel. Nehemiah 12:1–21 therefore contains a list of priests and Levites going back to the period in the late part of the sixth century B.C.E. (Jeshua, named in verse 1, was high priest in 520) and stretching forward to the time of king Alexander the Great (Jaddua, named in verse 11, was high priest in 323). The list concludes with the names of temple singers and gatekeepers (vv. 24–25), and with a final reference weaves together the names of three individuals of different periods: "These were in the days of Joiakim son of Jeshua son of Jozadak, and in the days of the governor Nehemiah and of the priest Ezra, the scribe" (v. 26). Unity of purpose—in rebuilding and reclaiming the temple, in restoring the city as the extension of the house of God, and in reforming the community under the guidance of the Torah—marks the activity of the restoration period with which the names of Joiakim, Nehemiah, and Ezra are associated.

A HOUSEWARMING
Nehemiah 12:27—13:3

Dedication of the Wall (12:27–43)

12:27 Now at the dedication of the wall of Jerusalem they sought out the Levites in all their places, to bring them to Jerusalem to celebrate the

dedication with rejoicing, with thanksgivings and with singing, with cymbals, harps, and lyres. [28] The companies of the singers gathered together from the circuit around Jerusalem and from the villages of the Netophathites; [29] also from Beth-gilgal and from the region of Geba and Azmaveth; for the singers had built for themselves villages around Jerusalem. [30] And the priests and the Levites purified themselves; and they purified the people and the gates and the wall.

With the house in order, the time has come for a celebration. In this passage we note again the predominance of the word *Jerusalem*. Those inside the city come together for the celebration, and those outside come to Jerusalem to participate. Music is an important aspect of the festivities, and both singers and instruments are therefore listed. Then priests and Levites purify themselves and everyone around them, including the gates and the wall, to make them ready for participation in the procession and thanksgiving that follow.

The entire celebration is called "the dedication of the wall of Jerusalem" (v. 27). In Hebrew the word for dedication is *hanukkah*. As the temple had been dedicated earlier (Ezra 6:16–18), so the wall is dedicated at this time. Sacrifices are offered to signify that this is an occasion for marking a space as holy, just as it was done at the dedication of the temple (Ezra 6:17). Is the Jewish celebration of Hanukkah a commemoration of these *hanukkahs* at the time of Ezra and Nehemiah? Actually, the feast of Hanukkah goes back to a period when the temple was rededicated after the forces of assimilation had compromised its purity in the second century B.C.E. when Judah was a part of the Greek empire. The struggle for the Jewish community to maintain itself as a distinct ethnic and religious group would ebb and flow for centuries after Ezra and Nehemiah. The pressure to become like others around them, to assimilate to the culture, was especially strong during the period of the empire established after Alexander the Great (332 B.C.E.), with its dominant culture of Hellenism. Persecution and torture of those who refused to succumb to Hellenist influence took place in the early decades of the second century, and a violent reaction was the result under the leadership of Judas Maccabaeus. After the temple was reclaimed successfully, it was rededicated, and a feast was held marked by the placing of lights especially in the temple square; hence the lighting of the Menorah during the observation of Hanukkah today.

In verse 31 the narrative switches back to the first person, and Nehemiah moves to the foreground with Ezra in the picture with him. Each leads one half of the people. The exact route taken by the procession is not clear, because we no longer are familiar with all of the locations. The movement is, however, clearly of two groups of people, moving in opposite directions on the city walls to meet eventually in one place at the temple. "One went to the right. . . . The other company . . . went to the left" (vv. 31 and 38). Ezra heads up one line, Nehemiah follows the other (vv. 36 and 38).

Responses of Great Joy (12:40–43)

12:40 So both companies of those who gave thanks stood in the house of God, and I and half of the officials with me; [41] and the priests Eliakim, Maaseiah, Miniamin, Micaiah, Elioenai, Zechariah, and Hananiah, with trumpets; [42] and Maaseiah, Shemaiah, Eleazar, Uzzi, Jehohanan, Malchijah, Elam, and Ezer. And the singers sang with Jezrahiah as their leader. [43] They offered great sacrifices that day and rejoiced, for God had made them rejoice with great joy; the women and children also rejoiced. The joy of Jerusalem was heard far away.

Both companies stand "in the house of God," that is to say, within the city walls, which is now sanctified space. Priests and singers all do their part, making sacrifices and giving voice. The people here include even the women and the children, explicitly present only on a few other occasions in the Ezra-Nehemiah material. The last verse overflows with words for rejoicing and joy.

We may safely assume this celebration to have been a noisy, exuberant, and rambunctious affair. The text states that "the joy of Jerusalem was heard far away." The book of Lamentations compares this very city after the Exile to a bereaved and wounded woman who found no comfort anywhere; over whom the enemy gloated and the singers mourned. The joy that is heard "far away" needs to be viewed also in that context. Lamentation has turned to joy; the distress that was the last word of the confessional prayer in Nehemiah 9 has changed to gladness. Even on the occasion of restoring the foundations of the temple, gladness was mixed with weeping at the rejoicing, then too heard "far away" (Ezra 4:13). At this completion of the restoration of temple, city, and community, there is only unalloyed rejoicing. The words of Isaiah spoken before the imminent return of the exiles come to mind: "So the ransomed of the LORD shall return, and come to Zion with singing" (Isa. 51:11).

Liturgical celebrations in our own context, like those at Easter for example, are usually more reserved and formalized than what is described here. But we may remember a moment when for us too the ritual broke through the limits put on it by the liturgy. I think back to a service of worship held in our Seminary chapel a few years ago, when the entire congregation during the final singing rose to its feet and began to march through the sanctuary, singing and processing in a swinging dancing line, for the joy in our hearts could not be contained and caused our bodies to move with our spirits. Those are celebrations that happen only occasionally, and we cherish and remember them for a long time.

Fulfillment of a Pledge (12:44–47)

The last section in this chapter records the fulfillment of agreements taken on for the upkeep of the temple and those who serve it (vv. 44–47). The link with the past is firmly maintained by connecting the activities of temple personnel with regulations made in the days of king David: "They performed the service of their God and the service of purification, as did the singers and the gatekeepers, according to the command of David and his son Solomon. For in the days of David and Asaph long ago there was a leader of the singers, and there were songs of praise and thanksgiving to God" (Neh. 12:45–46). In verses 44–47 the appropriateness of music and singing receives special emphasis with words for rejoicing and singing appearing in each verse. "All Israel" joins in the task taken on to continue the joyful practices of the past. These practices may have been broken off, but this break proved to be only an interruption, and they can be resumed. Those who have sown in tears now indeed reap with shouts of joy (Ps. 126:5).

Separation—A Mark of Identity (13:1–3)

13:1 **On that day they read from the book of Moses in the hearing of the people; and in it was found written that no Ammonite or Moabite should ever enter the assembly of God, 2 because they did not meet the Israelites with bread and water, but hired Balaam against them to curse them—yet our God turned the curse into a blessing. 3 When the people heard the law, they separated from Israel all those of foreign descent.**

Three times in these last passages the words "on that day" are repeated (Neh. 12:43, 44, and 13:1). This term sets up special reverberations within the biblical text. The prophet Amos uses these words, for example, as code words for a day to come, also called "the day of the Lord," when God will bring final judgment (Amos 8:9–14) or, conversely, final salvation (Amos

9:11–15). "The days (or "the time") is coming" are words used with similar connotations. (Amos 8:11; 9:13; Jer. 31:31, for example.) The descriptions that follow such opening words call up climactic moments. "That day" in Nehemiah 12 and 13 marks a day of celebration (12:43), of following through on responsibilities (12:44), and in chapter 13, verse 1, of emphasis on the identity of the community that engages in these activities. "That day" is here indeed a day of culmination of all the efforts of restoration that have punctuated this period. As such, as the acme of all that was hoped for, it is also set in a direct line with an earlier time by the words "in those days," words that are then drawn forward by the phrase "the days of Zerubbabel and . . . Nehemiah" (12:47).

The final mention of "that day" is distinguished by a reading from the Torah. Texts relevant to the concern about Ammonite and Moabite presence can be found in Numbers 21–23 and Deuteronomy 23:3–6. We visit these occasions of a desire for emphatic separation on the part of the community with uneasiness. It seems at first as if the excluded groups will be limited to the specified nationalities, but the final phrase extends the separation to "all those of foreign descent" (13:3). Yet the very law that forbade admission of Ammonites and Moabites to the congregation specifically includes people of Edomite and Egyptian descent (Deut. 23:7–8). Laws dealing with separating ancient Israel from its neighbors are complex and ambiguous and are contradicted by the pervasive concern and love for the stranger in the Torah. (Deut. 1:16; 16:19; 19:19; 24:17; Lev. 19:34, for example.) Nehemiah 13:3 expands the relatively few Torah laws on restricting intercourse with outsiders and makes them more stringent and exclusive.

Desire and need for identity expressed in the Ezra-Nehemiah texts versus the demand for hospitality produces tensions that are not always resolved in a manner that meets with our approval. We need a reminder that our disapproval of such practices must go accompanied by a close look at the actions of our Christian community that spell exclusion and separation from groups and races. Perhaps we are more inclusive by the book and more exclusive in practice than we think. Second, we must keep in mind the gigantic struggle for survival in which the Jewish community of this period was engaged, a struggle that went on for centuries. Last, perhaps the community of this period is depicted as more separatist than it was in reality, more exclusive by the book and more inclusive in practice. Certainly, what follows in Nehemiah seems to bear this out (Neh. 13:23–27).

FURTHER HOUSECLEANING
Nehemiah 13:4–31

Another Troubled Arrival (13:4–14)

13:4 Now before this, the priest Eliashib, who was appointed over the chambers of the house of our God, and who was related to Tobiah, 5 prepared for Tobiah a large room where they had previously put the grain offering, the frankincense, the vessels, and the tithes of grain, wine, and oil, which were given by commandment to the Levites, singers, and gatekeepers, and the contributions for the priests. 6 While this was taking place I was not in Jerusalem, for in the thirty-second year of King Artaxerxes of Babylon I went to the king. After some time I asked leave of the king 7 and returned to Jerusalem. I then discovered the wrong that Eliashib had done on behalf of Tobiah, preparing a room for him in the courts of the house of God. 8 And I was very angry, and I threw all the household furniture of Tobiah out of the room. 9 Then I gave orders and they cleansed the chambers, and I brought back the vessels of the house of God, with the grain offering and the frankincense.

One could wish that Nehemiah's book had ended with chapter 12. The last episodes are filled with turbulence and antagonism and report some actions on Nehemiah's part that strike us as outrageous. With the reappearance of Nehemiah in a first person account, the story regains a personal and very human touch. The last activities of Nehemiah are distinguished by his efforts as governor to administer correct implementation of agreements made by the people. It appears as if the text again opens with a time marker, "before this." It is also possible to translate the Hebrew with "in the face of this" or "in view of this." That is to say, in view of all that had gone on, agreements and celebrations, Nehemiah was faced with certain tasks. However we understand the term, what becomes clear and what is most important is that the reestablishment of the community, reclaiming the house of God and itself as a house of God, is a process that is never finished. To end the account with the reports of chapter 12 would provide a somewhat unreal picture and a false impression of "All's well that ends well." Instead, the writer recounts further struggles to implement restoration efforts, thus ending the Ezra-Nehemiah work in a way that opens it up to the future. The effort of rebuilding itself on the part of the Jewish community will be ongoing, will have its ups and downs, its joys and sorrows. In the end, its survival will be nothing short of miraculous.

First, and directly counter to the provisions taken in the section immediately preceding, an Ammonite is found within the temple precincts! We meet here our old friend Tobiah once more, the one who in previous accounts had caused Nehemiah no end of trouble (Neh. 2:10; 4:3; chap. 6 throughout). He was identified elsewhere as an Ammonite and also as related by family to the community in Judah. Troublesome, as before, is the alliance of a member of the community, this time a priest no less, with the very same enemy of Nehemiah.

In the course of the story we find out that Nehemiah was at the Persian court at the time that Tobiah finds lodging in the temple precincts. The year indicated in verse 6, "the thirty-second year of King Artaxerxes of Babylon," would place Nehemiah's absence in 432, twelve years *after* the dedication celebrations. The reading "before this" of verse 4 becomes more problematic in view of the dates provided. Exact date lines and time sequences are not the main point of the author, however. I suggest that we understand the period of Nehemiah's ongoing "housecleaning" to be taking place after the activities recorded in chapters 12 and 13:1–3, but not to become fixated on precise dating. The main point of the story is to tell of a *process* of restoration; this process we need to keep in view.

The reported stay of Nehemiah at the king's court, mentioned almost as an aside in verse 6, raises interesting questions about Nehemiah's obligations. Was his tenure as governor ended, and did he seek renewal? Or were such trips for administrative purposes regular ones? How long did he stay in Persia? If the trip took a total of six months, going and coming, then he was away for more than half a year. Certainly, this would have been enough time to install Tobiah in the temple quarters. The potential conflict residing in Nehemiah's representing both the Persian government and the Jewish community resurfaces with this one mention of Nehemiah's return trip to Babylon. The room prepared for Tobiah was intended as a storage room for the required contributions to the temple. It is not clear whether these contributions are lacking or whether they are simply stored elsewhere. Grain offering, vessels, and frankincense are put back by Nehemiah, but no mention is made in verse 9 of the rest of the provisions.

Once Nehemiah had arrived in Jerusalem from Persia to find broken walls (Neh. 2:11–16); this time he encounters what is in his view a broken community. When Nehemiah discovers what has gone on behind his back, he has a temper tantrum, throwing all of Tobiah's belongings out of the room. This part of the story reveals a degree of exasperation and a temperament on the part of Nehemiah that sounds almost comic. We can see him heaving chairs, tables, and clothes out into the hallway. Where Tobiah was at the time, the text does not reveal.

It is true that Nehemiah is present in the material named after him in all his conflicted humanity. He has just been on a journey to the king of Persia, the one who had ultimate authority over his person and his people and to whom he must give account for his governorship. The king had probably summoned him, and he needs to ask for permission to return to Jerusalem (v. 6). The Persian administration had an interest in keeping things stable in the provinces, and Nehemiah had in all likelihood given an optimistic account of the situation in Judah and Jerusalem. He trusted that all would go well back home during his absence, and now this! Even if Nehemiah's actions toward Tobiah were motivated to a degree by personal animosity, there is no reason to doubt his devotion to the temple. His actions may remind us of a later day when Jesus removes forcibly from the temple precinct what he considered to be polluting elements. (See Matt. 21:12–13; Mark 11:15–17; Luke 19:45–46; John 2:13–17.)

Verses 10–14 bear out that the room made ready for use by Tobiah may indeed not have been as stocked as it should have been with the provisions pledged at one time. Levites and singers have stopped serving the temple and have actually gone back to their farms! "Why," Nehemiah reproaches the leaders of the community, "is the house of God forsaken?" (v. 11). The word "forsaken" links the concern directly to the pledge taken up at the end of chapter 9 that consisted in a promise not to "neglect" the house of God. In Hebrew the words translated with "forsaken" and "neglect" are the same.

Chapter 13:4–31 takes up the three areas of agreement entered into by the community, in reverse order from the way they were presented in chapter 9. First Nehemiah addresses the issue of tithes for the temple, next he challenges the breaking of sabbath laws, and last he takes up mixed marriages. The reality was that the community may have been ill equipped in terms of all three areas. Many of the people were poor, and tithing may have become too heavy a burden; not working on the sabbath meant loss of income; the people are not numerous, and the presence of many different ethnic groups in the area would make it tempting to expand the community by intermarriage.

Keeping the Sabbath Holy (13:15–22)

Verses 15–22 describe how things have gone wrong on the sabbath and the measures taken by Nehemiah to rectify the situation. People are engaging in trade and buying from outsiders (vv.15–16). So Nehemiah, after berating a group of leaders, has guards posted on gates that remain shut throughout the sabbath to enforce the agreement once made voluntarily

(Neh. 10:31). An enforced agreement does not strike us as having the same value as a voluntary one. On the other hand, we recognize that at times the only way to make agreements work is to enforce them.

Each time Nehemiah finds a flaw in the conduct of the people he becomes involved physically or threatens to do so. He "throws" the furniture of Tobias out of the temple room, threatens to "lay hands" on the merchants outside the city gates, and on the third occasion he does lay hands on the perpetrators of the offense. This last episode of the book is full of turmoil. Apart from reasons already mentioned that would make intermarriage an attractive practice, so strict a fence around the covenant community had not been a feature of the people before the Exile. When the Jewish community of Ezra and Nehemiah's time heard the Torah, they also listened to stories in which outsiders were adopted into the family of Israel without question. They heard laws that provided for just and loving treatment of strangers. The laws that forbade marriage with non-Israelites are few, and they are concentrated in a particular section of the Torah, Deuteronomy. So there must have been some people who felt that there were other directions taken in ancient times than those that excluded all of foreign descent and that therefore other directions were possible for them.

Keeping the People Separate (13:23–28)

Faced with the third element of disaster, the issue of mixed marriages, Nehemiah becomes more vehement and physically assaults the perpetrators of the offense: "And I contended with them and cursed them and beat some of them and pulled out their hair; and I made them take an oath in the name of God, saying, "You shall not give your daughters to their sons, or take their daughters for your sons or for yourselves" (Neh.13:25). This is certainly a strange and off-putting picture. Nehemiah is not a leader who convinces by tact and political maneuvering. His approach is direct, physical, and threatening. There is little here to admire. Yet the lack of behind-the-scenes manipulation has at least the quality of honesty. In addition, we note that Nehemiah, unlike Ezra, takes no measure to expel anyone from the community. He simply forbids such irregular behavior for the future and sounds more like an exasperated parent than a political leader. Such behavior and threats, also on the part of parents, are often futile.

Futility proves to be the case in the next verses, where it appears that intermarrying with outsiders has taken place inside the high priestly family (Neh. 13:28). This particular offense is all the more galling for Nehemiah because it concerns Sanballat, another one of his enemies. Nehemiah "chased him away," but how far away is not clear. The text makes no mention of expulsion from the community. Two of Nehemiah's archenemies have surfaced in this episode, and one doubts somehow that these are gone for good.

A Prayer for Remembrance (13:29–31)

13:29 **Remember them, O my God, because they have defiled the priesthood, the covenant of the priests and the Levites.**

30 **Thus I cleansed them from everything foreign, and I established the duties of the priests and Levites, each in his work;** 31 **and I provided for the wood offering, at appointed times, and for the first fruits. Remember me, O my God, for good.**

Verse 29 is reminiscent of earlier prayers for vengeance on his enemies by Nehemiah (Neh. 4:4; 6:14). The second prayer is in his own behalf (v. 31). The plea for remembrance addressed to God in the Bible always means more than a simple calling to mind. When believers in ancient Israel called on God to "remember" them, the plea is for God to turn toward someone or the community with gracious, liberative action (Pss. 25:7; 74:2; 106:4; 119:49; 132:1). Occasionally, believers petition God to "remember" the enemy (Ps. 137:7). In that case, the desired action taken by God is destructive. Even though verse 29 does not spell out the nature of the punishment taken, it is safe to assume that punishment is precisely what Nehemiah has in mind.

The prayers are linked by a short list of credits. Nehemiah, who was also the representative of the foreign government, wants to go down in history for what he did in behalf of his community as a member of that community. He had originally come from Persia to repair the city walls and had acquitted himself well. In this last chapter he occupies himself with repair of the community. Some of us might think he should have stuck to building programs, but Nehemiah may have been desirous to prove himself worthy in other ways. Rather than self-righteous, Nehemiah strikes one as uncertain—uncertain of his standing with the community, uncertain of his standing with God.

And so the story ends, although it is far from over. In the final scenes we meet an all too human and frustrated leader who sees much of what was accomplished gone awry. Nehemiah and his community are both full of imperfections. For such leaders and such communities as they are, as we are, Nehemiah's prayer may not be inappropriate: "Remember us, O our God, for good."

Esther

Introduction

Many of us probably remember Esther and know the book named for her, at least in general outline. The trouble with a well-remembered tale can be that we do not know it as well as we think. The story goes that once upon a time the Jews were threatened with destruction and Esther saved the day. Or was it Mordecai who turned the danger around? Haman we may remember as a despicable character who got what he deserved. A king with a difficult name plays a part too. When did all this happen exactly? Perhaps we recall a connection with the Purim festival. In my youth, Esther was favorite Sunday School material. From those recollections Mordecai comes especially to mind, dressed up and riding on a horse. That feature of the story must have been illustrated vividly, perhaps with the figures of felt made to stick on felt, beloved of Sunday School teachers everywhere.

One of the reasons for some vagueness about the book of Esther may be that it never made it out of the Sunday School into the pulpit or became a subject for serious Bible study. In addition, Esther is in many ways a difficult book that raises some questions for which there are no easy answers. Great conflict unfolds in this text, and the book raised conflict in the religious communities to which it belongs. What type of story is the book of Esther? What is it about? Whence did it originate? What sort of difficulties does it present to the community of faith? Who are the major characters? These questions we review before we begin our study in closer detail.

ONCE UPON A TIME . . .

The Bible contains many kinds of stories, many of which connect directly to a historical period. We can think, for example, of 1 and 2 Samuel, 1 and 2 Kings, or Ezra and Nehemiah. We could call such biblical texts "historical narrative," because they present the story of the people of ancient Israel in certain historical periods. We use the word "narrative" because the stories are told in a fashion akin to what we identify today as fiction rather than history. In the texts about king David, for example, we get to know him as a very human character with his ups and downs, his virtues and his failings. The account of his family, with its intimate details, does not fit the category of history. Ezra and Nehemiah are present in the material named for them as individuals with their feelings, hopes, and fears recorded, as well as their activities. The writer of Ezra-Nehemiah, on the other hand, is not a historian who is interested in getting all the historical dates lined up precisely.

The word *historical* applies insofar as such stories refer directly to historical events that took place in the biblical era. Often we know also of these events from documents outside of the Bible. Yet history written in the Bible is not like history as we encounter it today in a history book. To us, an account does not seem true if it cannot be verified by historical facts. The question "Is it true?" for us equals the question "Did it really happen?" For the biblical writers, truth does not rest primarily in historically verifiable facts. The stories of the Bible convey truth about God's engagement with the community and the community's response to that engagement. God's dealings with the people and their response to God's guidance took place in history, and the biblical stories are therefore also a reflection of that history. The historical realities that form the context for a given biblical narrative are always important for consideration.

The book of Esther is more clearly *narrative* than *history*. It is a "Once upon a time" story set in the days of a Persian king called Ahasuerus, usually understood to be King Xerxes I or Artaxerxes II, rulers in the fifth and fourth centuries B.C.E. The events take place at the Persian court and in the empire at large. The overriding reality of the story is the threat to the survival of the Jewish community that lives in the realm. This reality is more appropriate for a period later than the one provided by "the days of Ahasuerus" (Esther 1:1). It is possible that the actual context of Esther is the persecution of the Jews that took place under Antiochus IV Epiphanes in the first quarter of the second century B.C.E. The reality of the threat to Jewish survival and its miraculous reversal is the truth conveyed by Esther. This truth is told in the form of a folk story marked by exaggeration and the one-dimensional features of its characters. Exaggeration is evident from the length of the royal party in the opening chapter (Esther 1:1–9), from the height of the gallows (Esther 5:14), and from the immutability of the king's decrees (Esther 1:19; 8:8). The characters are undeveloped and remain one-dimensional, representing foolishness (the king), evil (Haman), good (Mordecai), and beauty (Esther). Esther is the only character to show development and change, and thereby stands out from the rest of the cast of more static personalities.

A general period from the early fifth to the early second century B.C.E. allows the widest possible margins for the time in which the book of Esther may have been composed. About the writer we can say with certainty that this was a skillful artist who wrote with a strong sense of irony. Although the Jews were not actively persecuted during this entire period, Jewish identity and survival were major concerns at this time. If the historical background for Esther is identified with the first part of the second century B.C.E., the Jews lived indeed endangered lives. At that time, the ruler, Antiochus IV Epiphanes, attempted to force assimilation on the Jews. He put to torture and death those who refused to participate in Hellenized religious rites and those who insisted on maintaining Jewish practices such as Torah reading, circumcision, and keeping the food laws. Many of the Jews in Judah must have felt that their community was finally coming to an end. Against this dark background, we may view Esther as a subversive story that mocked those in power who are finally outwitted by a most unlikely rescuer.

The community in the book of Esther lives in Persia. Whether we adopt the historical dating for Esther suggested here or assign it to an earlier period, the truth was that the Jews lived a precarious existence from the Babylonian Exile on. Their life as a distinct ethnic religious group was far from assured, whether at home in Judah or abroad in the Persian empire. If they assimilated to the dominant culture, their identity was in danger; if they separated themselves strongly from their surroundings, their difference made them more vulnerable to violent interference. In the Esther story it is the distinctive identity of the Jews in an alien land that opens them up to persecution. It is their difference that Haman points out to the king when he convinces the king to go along with his plot (Esther 3:8). Separation is a liability in Esther. Yet Esther ends with survival and celebration. For the Jewish community, across years of renewed persecutions, Esther provides hope of victory against the odds.

As a Christian community, we look at the book of Esther through the screen of centuries of Christian persecution of the Jews. To us, as a post-Holocaust community, the story of the threat to "annihilate all Jews, young and old, women and children" (Esther 3:13) creates dreadful echoes. "Once upon a time . . . " became the days of Adolf Hitler, and the folktale turned into a horror story. Insofar as Christians share the burden of responsibility for the attempted mass murder of all the Jews in the Second World War, Esther affords an opportunity to look at the face of prejudice and persecution as in a mirror. Furthermore, Esther provides us with an occasion to contemplate the religious significance of Jewish survival. God, who is depicted in the Bible as being in intimate relation with this people, must be involved with the ongoing existence of the covenant community. It matters to God that the decree of annihilation issued against the Jews is overturned. In addition, the descendants of ancient Israel eventually gave birth to the faith of Judaism and Christianity. How these two groups relate to one another is a religious question. Christianity has traditionally denied the validity of Judaism and has seen itself as the rightful successor of ancient Israel. Esther may teach us anew about the legitimacy of Judaism and provide us with tools to redefine the relationship of the two faith groups.

In any case, the book of Esther is not "religious" in the traditional sense. It makes no reference to God. There is no mention of religious institutions such as the temple, or of assemblies for liturgical purposes, or of texts such as the Torah. Even prayer is not mentioned, not even when a fast is called, an event traditionally accompanied by prayer (Esther 4:16). If God is not a presence in the book, there is a presence that is all too evident. Esther as a tale is carnival-like, mocking, ridiculing, and eventually victimizing the victimizers, features death as a major player. Death stalks the festivities from beginning to end.

CONTROVERSY AROUND ESTHER

Such a story from which God is seemingly absent and in which important religious institutions and practices are not mentioned caused problems for the religious communities that viewed the Bible as their sacred Scripture. For the Jews who set limits to the biblical canon around the turn of the first century C.E., the lack of such references caused them to question the book of Esther's appropriateness for the Hebrew Bible. The main reason for keeping the story in the canon eventually was that the text provides a foundation for the festival of Purim (Esther 8—9). In the end, Esther was preserved in the biblical canon and the book was assigned to be read in the synagogue during the celebration of Purim on the fourteenth day of the month Adar (February or March of the Christian calendar). Today in the Jewish community, Purim is held as a feast of fun and practical jokes, with children dressed up as various characters in the story.

For Christians, the book of Esther provides some problems that were identical to the objections of the rabbis and some that were dissimilar.

Many prominent Christian scholars and church leaders have denounced Esther as a book that is too violent, and without reference to God, while its ostensible main point, the celebration of Purim, is a feast unfamiliar to the Christian community. Esther is simply too Jewish for Christian tastes. Christian folk do not really know what to do with Esther, and, although the story is firmly ensconced in the biblical canon, the story, which has been relegated to the Sunday School, has lost its significance. It is a known story, but a diminished story without value for the faith.

Yet there is much in the book of Esther to instruct believers. We learn here about the face of oppression: the oppression of the Jews in the diaspora and also the later Christian oppression of the Jewish community. By extension, the landscape of all systemic oppression and prejudice everywhere comes into view. The book of Esther shows where race prejudice leads. Esther herself, who was cut off from her people, provides an example of liberation through solidarity with victims of oppression. Her stand is all the more valiant because it is not taken heedlessly but after much hesitation and demurral.

The book of Esther is also about sexism, the ideology of patriarchy. She is a member of a vulnerable class in three ways: as an orphan, a woman, and an alien who is a Jew. She functions as a female rescuer in the shadow of the banished queen Vashti. She is an alien who has to hide her particular Jewish identity. She is confined to the harem, which keeps her outside of the information loop. From Esther we learn also about the possibilities of overcoming the constraints designed by a patriarchal world and may discern the design of a pattern to overcome such constraints.

The book of Esther is about thumbing one's nose at the bully on the playground and about laughing at the ones who fall into the trap they set for others. The story provides a delicious sense of poetic justice with the villains getting what they deserve. It is, finally, a wonderfully entertaining story, skillfully told and captivating our interest, filled with laughter in the face of destruction.

PLOT AND CHARACTERS

The book of Esther contains nine chapters in which the story is introduced, developed, and brought to its conclusion. Three verses are added as an appendix to form a very brief tenth chapter. Chapters 1—3 introduce the setting, the main characters, and the plotline. The setting is the royal court where one queen vanishes to be replaced by another, where a plot is discovered against the king's life and another is constructed against the life of all the Jews. This last threat provides the danger to be overcome in the main section of the book, chapters 4—7. Successful mediation by a female member of the threatened community causes the downfall of the main schemer in the story and opens the way to a reversal of the fate of annihilation for the Jews. The setting alternates between the palace and the city of Susa. In the last episodes, chapters 8—9, the setting is the Jewish community. The Jews not only survive but decimate their enemies. In celebration of this event the festival of Purim is established.

Primary characters are king Ahasuerus and his adviser Haman, both Persians, and the Jews Mordecai and Esther. There is also a cast of minor characters, which includes other advisers to the king such as Memucan, a Persian official; Hegai and Hathach, eunuchs over the harem; and two other women, queen Vashti and Zeresh, the wife of Haman.

Ahasuerus represents *the* power in the Persian empire. As a character, he comes across consistently as weak, easy to manipulate, not too bright, at times completely bewildered and lacking in perspicacity. The storyteller pokes fun at the king whenever he is on the scene. The real power in this kingdom is wielded by Haman, who represents every schemer that ever worked an administration to his advantage. Haman is full of evil intent and a sense of self-inflated worth. He proves finally that a coward hides beneath his bullying exterior. Mordecai is the Jew who is the antagonist to Haman. Mordecai is introduced as a descendant of the house of Benjamin and related to king Saul. He is also the guardian of his cousin Esther. Throughout the story, Mordecai shows singleness of purpose—opposition to Haman and all that he stands for.

Esther represents beauty and charm in the opening chapters. She captivates all around her, including the eunuch in charge of the harem and the king himself. Initially, she hides her identity as a Jew at the court. As already noted, Esther is the only character to undergo change in the course of the narrative. From a charmer who hides her true self, she comes out of the shadows to claim her identity and to intercede successfully for her community. By overcoming the limits of her existence, she rises from power that is a sham to true power. She becomes someone when she is able to lay claim to who she is and in that capacity is able to save her people.

Minor characters function as a kind of foil for the principal ones and also as a vehicle to keep the story line moving. Memucan, as adviser to the king in the matter of queen Vashti in chapter 1, foreshadows Haman's role as main manipulator of king Ahasuerus (Esther 1:16–20). Vashti anticipates Esther in her independence. Her fate, in addition, provides the somber reality of consequences that may follow taking an independent stand. Esther plays her role of mediator against this background. Her statement "if I perish, I perish" shows her awareness of this reality (Esther 4:16). The eunuchs Hegai and Hathach afford Esther with opportunities in terms of her access to the king and her communication with Mordecai (Esther 2:8–9 and 4:5–11). Zeresh, Haman's wife, functions as a type of adviser to her husband. Ironically, the gallows erected for Mordecai by Haman, on her advice, becomes the means for Haman's execution (Esther 5:14 and 7:9–10).

Besides these, there are groups of characters with specific functions everywhere: advisers, servants, and secretaries. Some of these are named, some remain anonymous. They help the plot along by carrying out orders or by disclosing important information. We turn now to the text itself to examine the details of what has been outlined here.

6. The Court of Ahasuerus
Esther 1—3

These first three chapters provide the setting and context for what is to follow. They open with a lavish party at king Ahasuerus' court in Persia that goes on for months (Esther 1:1–9). Parties punctuate the book with great regularity. The first party is the largest and most ostentatious and it ends in the banishment of queen Vashti when she refuses to come into the king's presence (Esther 1:10–20). Merriment permeated with conflict is typical for the sequel and is thus introduced efficiently in the first chapter. The second chapter introduces a search for a new queen and brings on the scene Mordecai and Esther, his cousin and ward, both Jews (Esther 2:1–7). Esther becomes a candidate as a replacement for queen Vashti and by luck and skill finds favor with the king, so that he makes her queen (Esther 2:8–18). Directly following Esther's triumph and the party given in her favor is an account of Mordecai's discovery of a plot against the king's life. This becomes known to the king via Esther, and the villains are hanged. The second party in the book thus goes accompanied by an execution (Esther 2:23). Chapter 3 introduces the fourth main character of the book in the person of Haman. Haman is elevated to a powerful position at the court. Mordecai immediately crosses him, and Haman is thus provoked to plan the annihilation not only of Mordecai but of all his people (Esther 3:1–6). This plot is set in motion by Haman's skillful manipulation of his royal master, and the decree of the impending destruction is announced in all the provinces (Esther 3:7–15). The scene concludes with the king and his adviser refreshing themselves with drink and the city reportedly in turmoil (Esther 3:15).

A QUEEN VANISHES
Esther 1

A Royal Party (1:1–12)

1:1 **This happened in the days of Ahasuerus, the same Ahasuerus who ruled over one hundred twenty-seven provinces from India to Ethiopia. ² In those**

days when King Ahasuerus sat on his royal throne in the citadel of Susa, 3 in the third year of his reign, he gave a banquet for all his officials and ministers. The army of Persia and Media and the nobles and governors of the provinces were present, 4 while he displayed the great wealth of his kingdom and the splendor and pomp of his majesty for many days, one hundred eighty days in all.

The book opens with a lavish party of a duration that is difficult to imagine. If this were indeed King Xerxes, it is hard to believe that a successful ruler such as he had time to take half the year off for a party. Not only that, but all the important administrators of his realm are present as well. One hundred twenty-seven provinces are without governors for 180 days. The extravagant presentation of the king and his party entourage serves to introduce him as perhaps not a very responsible person. Yet he is the king, his empire is large, he has much wealth to display, so he can throw as large a party as he wants.

When all the important people have seen all there is to be seen, the population of Susa is invited for another celebration. They are all served well and are allowed to admire the beautiful appointments of the palace (1:5–6). On this occasion drinking is mentioned specifically; in fact, drinking is said to be "without restraint" (v. 8). Such imbibing will have its effects on the king, as well as the guests. Almost as an afterthought, queen Vashti is introduced; she is having a party of her own, for the women.

As was to be expected, the effects of too much alcohol make themselves felt, for the king is said to be "merry with wine" (v. 10). Not quite drunk, but certainly not sober, the king has an idea. He invites the queen to appear before him and everyone else, to show off her beauty. Actually, the invitation sounds more like an order: "He commanded . . . to bring" (vv. 10–11). The queen returns an unqualified refusal, and the king's happy mood turns to anger. "At this the king was enraged, and his anger burned within him" (v. 12). It is clear that the king drinks too much and moves too quickly from one mood to another. The refusal of queen Vashti may not have been polite, but it was hardly cause for rage.

What to say of Queen Vashti? Was she invited to appear without her clothes and dressed "only" in her crown as people often speculate? The text does not really provide that information. The information we are given is that Vashti gave her own party. It seems the most obvious to assume that she was simply too busy and did not feel like being absent as hostess from her guests. She was, in any case, not willing to jump at the king's word. Did she know the risk she took? The text does not say. We never get to meet Vashti, for she vanishes from the scene almost as soon as she appears. One may regret not getting to know her better. She seems, at least, to have a mind and a will of her own.

A Master in His House (1:13–22)

The rage of the king needs an outlet. The error of Vashti may have been an error of manners only, but something large needs to be done for him to feel satisfied. A small matter becomes bigger because of a reaction that is out of proportion to the offense. We will have occasion to meet this phenomenon again. So the king has a consultation with his advisers and asks them what the law has to say about Vashti's behavior. This is an odd question for one who ought to know the law of his own empire. But the question is hardly a real one. It works in its own way and provides an opening for one of the advisers to work out something creative. An official named Memucan makes the matter larger yet by stating that Vashti offended not only against the king but against everyone. He asserts that all women will get to hear of this uppityness and start to imitate her behavior. "Why," says Memucan, "This very day the noble ladies of Persia and Media who have heard of the queen's behavior will rebel against the king's officials, and there will be no end of contempt and wrath!" (Esther 1:18). That sort of thing obviously must be nipped in the bud. So Memucan advises to have a decree issued throughout the empire that Vashti may never come again into the king's presence and that she will be replaced as queen. That way all the women will fall into line. As if in anticipation of her downfall, Memucan refers to the queen without her title (v. 19).

Without further ado, the king has the decree sent out with the declaration that "every man should be master in his own house" (v. 22). Vashti, who did not want to come into the king's presence, now is forbidden to come into his presence! "Well then, if you don't want to come, you may never come again. So there!" What happened to Vashti we cannot know exactly. Was she banished to live out her life in another part of the harem? Was she exiled? Was she executed? The matter is left obscure. It is clear only that she loses her position as queen. Hers was a power apparently very easy to lose. The ambiguity of her fate has something threatening about it in itself; it was as if no one really cared what happened to her, once she was banished.

Of course, the punishment is ludicrously out of proportion to the offense. Memucan skillfully manipulates the king and every man's fears by dragging in potential misbehavior of other women. Then the entire administrative apparatus is set in motion to deal with this matter. What cost, what huffing and puffing to come to the grand conclusion that "every man should be master in his own house!" Surely the men of Persia in that day were masters in their house? Surely king Ahasuerus was master in his house? Or was he? The final phrase of the chapter throws into question exactly what it tries to assert.

In tone and content, the chapter is a fitting prelude for what is to come. Everything is out of proportion: the length of the banquet, the drinking, the accoutrements, the king's reaction to Vashti's refusal, and especially the consequences of her behavior. The king is depicted as self-indulgent, impulsive, swinging quickly from one mood to the next, and a prime candidate for manipulation by his servants. The servants, especially in the person of Memucan, are ready to take advantage of their master and move him to their ends.

The farcical presentation of much of what goes on here has, however, a dark undertone. Vashti disappears from the story almost as soon as she is introduced. Her queenly power meant nothing at all. Over her party falls the dark curtain of the uncertainty of her fate. This theme of tragedy in the midst of partying also anticipates events in the future.

Is it true? Did all this really happen? Taken at face value, a Persian king gave a lavish party in 483 B.C.E. There are some elements in these opening scenes, however, that do not fit the time and place of which the text speaks. As observed already, it is highly unlikely that an able ruler, as Xerxes is known to have been, would take such a long time off from his duties and responsibilities. The number of 127 provinces is not in agreement with the size of the Persian Empire as we know it. Also, the name of Xerxes' queen was Amestris, not Vashti. If the story were written a long time after the setting that is constructed for it, then the writer would feel a good degree of freedom to design events according to what fits the rest of the tale. The setting is partly make-believe with everything overstated to underline the extravagance and outrageous behavior of foreign rulers. An outsized party ends in an outsized reaction to a petty offense. Certainly it sounded familiar to those who suffered at the hands of the same extravagant and often capricious rulers in ancient Judah.

The truth is that there is much here for us to recognize. A man with too much money, too much time, too much power is thwarted in his desire for total control. Ahasuerus is like a peacock who cannot get enough of having others admire his display. He sets no limits to his showing off; everything and everyone is *his* after all. When someone else provides a limit, it enrages him and the party is over. It is especially aggravating that this someone is his wife, who has no real power of her own. Vashti is the subject of two verbs in the text: she "gave a banquet" (1:9), and she "refused to come at the king's command" (1:12). Her own party was not thrown by the king's command, and she refuses to budge when he calls. It is not surprising that the episode ends in reassertion of male control.

The mention of Vashti's party is one of two times in this book that women are mentioned as a group together with activities of their own. Does it irk the king that Vashti is secluded with other women? The text does not say what the king thought of it, but it is not unlikely that this party, held off to the side, worried him. Who knows what they are up to, these women, having their own good time, talking together and laughing! They are laughing at him most likely! And this is the company that Vashti actually prefers to that of her royal husband and master!

Although we are far removed in time and space from the setting of the story, there is little here that lies outside of our acquaintance. The setting of the book of Esther introduces also a very familiar patriarchal context. Patriarchy literally means a structure in which the father is the master of the house. The opening scene of Esther establishes that no assault on male control over the house will be tolerated. It need hardly be stated how ironically this assertion functions in the rest of the narrative.

A QUEEN APPEARS
Esther 2

A New Plan (2:1–4)

Four introductory verses announce the plans for a replacement for queen Vashti (Esther 2:1–4). Reportedly, the king is no longer angry, and "he remembered Vashti and what she had done and what had been decreed against her" (v. 1.) Is the king sorry? Would he rather have his queen back? Perhaps, but that option is not open since the law banning Vashti from his presence was one not to be altered (1:19). Unalterable decrees are not known to have existed historically, but they form a significant recurring motif in Esther. Whatever the feelings of the king are, his servants are ready with a plan. They suggest that new candidates be sought to fill the harem so that the king will have a rich variety from which to choose a queen.

Esther in the Palace (2:5–11)

2:8 **So when the king's order and his edict were proclaimed, and when many young women were gathered in the citadel of Susa in custody of Hegai, Esther also was taken into the king's palace and put in custody of Hegai, who had charge of the women. [9] The girl pleased him and won his favor, and he quickly provided her with her cosmetic treatments and her portion of food,** and with seven chosen maids from the king's palace, and advanced her and her maids to the best place in the harem. [10] Esther did not reveal her people or her kindred, for Mordecai had charged her not to tell. [11] Every day Mordecai would walk around in front of the court of the harem, to learn how Esther was and how she fared.

Before the plan is put in motion, the story introduces Mordecai and Esther (2:5–7). Mordecai is presented as a Jew, together with his ancestry, which places him in the line of Kish of the house of Benjamin. He is therefore related to king Saul. The precise significance of his ancestry will become evident as events develop. For now, the genealogy establishes Mordecai firmly as a person of importance. The next item of information is that he had taken on the guardianship of his cousin Esther, who is introduced both by her Jewish and her non-Jewish name. Esther is an orphan and is described as "fair and beautiful" (v. 7).

Esther is an obvious candidate for the pool that may provide a queen, so she finds herself in the harem, where she receives preferential treatment from the head eunuch, Hegai (vv. 8–9). At first, Esther is not the subject of any active verbs: "Mordecai adopted her," "Esther also was taken," and "put in custody of Hegai" (vv. 7–8). Then she is said to "please" Hegai and to have "won his favor" (v. 9). We conclude that she had an attractive character as well as physique. She gets people on her side, and they work in her behalf. All seems to be going well for Esther.

Verses 10 and 11 shed another light on life in the harem. Esther hides her identity on the instructions of her cousin and guardian. Mordecai himself is so concerned about her that he inquires daily how things are going for Esther and whether she is all right. Although the situation has turned out favorably for Esther, the overall impression we get is that she is winsome but also vulnerable.

We meet here Hegai, earlier called "the king's eunuch," who was in charge of the women. Eunuchs, who appeared already in chapter 1, where they were commissioned to "bring Queen Vashti before the king" (Esther 1:11), were castrated men who for obvious reasons were considered suitable to oversee the harem. They were also often powerful figures who could attain high status at the court. The authority of Hegai is underlined in verse 8 by a triple reference to his responsibility. Twice the text cites his "custody," besides the mention of his having "charge of the women." In fact, each reference to a eunuch in this chapter adds the reference to his responsibility for the women. Esther has no power accorded to her beyond her gift of beauty and talent of charm. She lives under the charge of the eunuch Hegai in the harem. Literally, the Hebrew states that she was "in the hand of Hegai" (v. 9).

A harem is a place closed off from the outside world. We notice that Mordecai has no direct contact with Esther but that he walks around, most likely inquiring of servants with access to the palace about Esther's welfare. There is traffic between the women in the harem and the king's rooms only, and even that only to a limited extent, as the following verses make clear. Mordecai certainly did not consider the harem a safe place for revealing one's Jewish identity. So, on Mordecai's instruction, Esther told no one that she was a Jew.

Esther's Turn (2:12–18)

A section follows on the customs of the harem. Details are provided of the beauty treatment received and the route the women followed after a night with the king. The women return to a second harem with another eunuch in charge; they make a return trip to the king's chambers only if they are "summoned by name" (Esther 2:14). If the harem, as is likely, had a large number of women, being remembered by name could become a problem!

The smooth presentation of the text hides the offensiveness of the customs described. "Each girl" takes a "turn" (v. 12). Waiting for her turn, she is an object for beautification. This wait amounts to a whole year, according to verse 12. These young women are under total control of the king via the eunuchs, in whose "hands" they literally have their existence.

Finally, Esther gets her "turn." It is noteworthy that this is one of two times that she is named together with the name of a parent (Esther 2:15 and 9:29). Abihail is a name that can be used of both sexes, so we cannot be sure whether her father or mother is indicated (see 1 Chron. 2:29, for example). Translated, the name means something like "my father is strength." Could this be a hint of the fact that there is more to Esther than meets the eye? There is also a reference to her prudence by the statement that she follows Hegai's advice as to what to take to the king's rooms (v. 15). This Esther certainly knows how to follow advice! Next, the text states that she "was admired by all who saw her" (v. 15), and the king is completely taken with her. "The king loved Esther more than all the other women; of all the virgins she won his favor and devotion, so that he set the royal crown on her head and made her queen instead of Vashti. Then the king gave a great banquet to all his officials and ministers—'Esther's banquet.' He also granted a holiday to the provinces, and gave gifts with royal liberality" (Esther 2:17–18).

It has taken a long time, for Esther is said to come to the king in "the seventh year of his reign" (v. 16). Since Vashti was banished in the king's third year, that makes a search of four years for a new queen. But now he has found her, and this one will not disobey him and refuse him her presence. Of that he will make sure. Because the king is by nature a party giver, a banquet concludes his choice of Esther as queen. The "royal crown" on her head may have been the very one Vashti had been expected to wear when she was invited. In any case, this is the last time Vashti is mentioned. A new day has arrived and with it a new queen. What we learn of Esther is that she is beautiful, is able to charm people, and does a very good job of following the instructions of the men in her surroundings. The expectation is created that such a woman will certainly not gainsay the king's command.

Mordecai's Service
to the King (2:19–23)

In a concluding section Mordecai helps uncover a plot against the king. The verses that introduce this section emphasize the presence of Mordecai near the palace (he is "sitting at the king's gate," v. 19) and reiterate the obedience of Esther to Mordecai's instructions in terms of her identity. She does as he tells her, just as when she still lived with him like his daughter (vv. 19–20). Because Mordecai is in a place where it is easy to pick up all kinds of gossip, he discovers a plot by two eunuchs to assassinate the king. On finding this out, Mordecai contrives to let Esther know; she lets the king know "in the name of Mordecai" (v. 22). The plot is uncovered, and the villains are executed. The text is careful to note the name of Mordecai at the point of the plot's revelation and the record kept of these events in the royal annals.

Eunuchs were often involved in court intrigue. Ahasuerus was not someone to endear himself to his entourage and may easily have aroused the ire of some of his servants. It could even be that Bigthan and Teresh, as the eunuchs are called, had a grudge against the king about the matter of Vashti. As was the case with Esther, Vashti may have had eunuchs who were loyal to her. However that may be, of importance is the service that Mordecai has rendered the king. Perhaps we may expect him soon to be in a more direct position to serve the king. The text sets up at least that expectation. Otherwise, here is a second party that is overshadowed by disaster. The king's life is not safe, and two would-be assassins find their death on the gallows.

We may wonder why Esther hid her identity. The text assigns the responsibility for her secrecy to Mordecai, and the question thus arises why Mordecai "charged her not to tell" (v. 10). The implication is certainly that he considered Esther's Jewishness to be a liability in the palace, and by allusion it is suggested that it is not safe to be a member of the Jewish people in this realm. It may have been a prudent decision on the part of Mordecai, but it is also one that puts an extra burden on Esther. Not revealing her identity means that she cannot keep the customs of her people, especially in terms of Jewish food laws. Esther is thus doubly isolated. She is cut off from her kindred in a physical sense by the enclosure of the harem; in addition, she is psychologically and spiritually separated from them. The new queen who has appeared is not her true self.

Such secrecy as Esther keeps is also detrimental in itself to the person who finds herself or himself in this position by force of circumstances. During the Second World War, Jews were literally and often figuratively forced into such hiding if they were intent on survival. Today, in many Christian communities gay and lesbian folk experience this forced cover-up of who they really are. The harm done by compelled existence "in the closet" is devastating. Esther, for example, has to be sure every moment that she measures up to standards she does not fully know and that are not set by the community of her natural alliance. She is "different" and must not let on to this difference at peril of her life.

There is danger abroad in this kingdom of splendor and grand feasts: danger to women who stand up for themselves; danger even to the highest power in the land; and danger especially for members of a certain community. Life is not stable in this environment. Is Mordecai attempting to shield himself, and Esther, from this threat by his service to the king? It is possible. How quickly the scales tip from a hidden to an open threat to the Jewish community becomes clear in the next chapter.

A DECREE FOR DESTRUCTION
Esther 3

The Promotion of Haman (3:1–6)

Chapter 3 can be divided into three sections. The first six verses provide background and setting for what follows. Time has passed, and Mordecai's service to the king is apparently forgotten, for the king appoints someone else to high office. This is the fourth main character that comes into focus in the book. His name is Haman, and he is introduced with his ancestry, like Mordecai. Mordecai's service to the king is overlooked, and another receives the highest possible honors. Not only is this the case, but Haman is introduced as a descendant of Agag, the Amalekite king, archenemy of king Saul. Since Mordecai is descended from the house of Saul, these two men are by their lineage set in opposition to one another. The honors heaped on Haman sound excessive; they include "obeisance," a full prostration rather than a bow (v. 2). The implied antagonism becomes outright hostility when Mordecai refuses to engage in this act of giving honor and respect.

The reason for Mordecai's refusal is not made explicit, but we may infer it from his implied opposition to Haman and from the interchange with the king's servants in the following verses (vv. 3–4). The servants fill the important function of providing crucial information at this point and act as go-betweens between the two main characters. They ask Mordecai why he goes against what is, after all, a royal command. When they push him on the issue without success, they tell Haman what Mordecai has told them, "that he was a Jew" (v. 4). We assume then that Mordecai himself gave this as the reason for his disobedience. It may have been more his lineage than his being a Jew that caused Mordecai to behave as he did, for bowing to those in authority was traditionally not forbidden to Mordecai's community (Gen. 23:7; 27:29; 1 Sam. 24:9, for example).

As Vashti's minor offense had caused a disproportionate reaction on the part of the king in the opening episode of the book, so Haman overreacts to Mordecai's behavior. In his rage, he plots to do away not just with Mordecai but with all his people. Verses 5 and 6 refer to Haman by name three times and four times to Mordecai. The sentences are filled with the names of these two to highlight their implacable opposition to one another.

Once again we encounter in the story the outsized negative response to a refusal from an inferior to behave as the one in control dictates. As with the case of Vashti and king Ahasuerus, the consequences that follow the offense extend to the entire group to which the offender belongs. But the farcical overtones that accompanied the royal decree against "all women" is missing from Haman's plans against "all the Jews" (v. 6). Also, Haman does not ask for anyone's advice, but he proceeds directly to set his plan in motion. Haman is far less ridiculous than his royal master and therefore far more dangerous.

Reprisals taken against a group because of a perceived offense perpetrated by an individual are a favorite means of intimidation and punishment by those who exercise tyrannical control over people. This type of action was habitual during the Second World War in countries that were occupied by Nazi Germany. Haman exceeds even tyrannical power by aiming for an entire people.

The Lot Is Cast (3:7–11)

3:8 Then Haman said to King Ahasuerus, "There is a certain people scattered and separated among the peoples in all the provinces of your kingdom; their laws are different from those of every other people, and they do not keep the king's laws, so that it is not appropriate for the king to tolerate them. 9 If it pleases the king, let a decree be issued for their destruction, and I will pay ten thousand talents of silver into the hands of those who have charge of the king's business, so that they may put it into the king's treasuries." 10 So the king took his signet ring from his hand and gave it to Haman son of Hammedatha the Agagite, the enemy of the Jews. 11 The king said to Haman, "The money is given to you, and the people as well, to do with them as it seems good to you."

In this second episode Haman prepares and executes the first parts of his plan. The lot is cast to determine a favorable time for the pogrom. Since *Pur* is not a Hebrew word, the writer translates it, retaining the word *Pur* in view of its obvious connection to *Purim*, the feast that will be the final outcome of these events. Feasting, however, is still a long way off for the Jews. By lot it is decided that their annihilation will take place on the twelfth month, almost a year from the time the lot is cast. The time span seems inordinately long but will serve its purposes in the story.

Next, Haman must convince the king of his plan. Verses 8–9 give the account of his argument. This is the first time that Haman is quoted directly; until now we have heard *about* him, not *from* him. Haman's speech is short; it consists of the motivation for the plan, the request for it, and the offer of the means to execute it. The motivation comes first, so that the request will have a firm foundation. In spite of its terseness, Haman's explanation is subtle and works up to its main point with a clever weaving together of some truths, some half-truths, some lies. He begins with an innocuous remark: "There is a certain people . . ." (v. 8). Well, that is true enough. The Persian Empire included many different ethnic groups, and in itself this observation would neither surprise nor startle the king. The next words are more disturbing, for Haman observes that these people, whoever they are, are everywhere: "scattered . . . in all the provinces of your kingdom," and they are "separated." They are not only everywhere, they keep themselves apart and are not really a part of the realm. That feature is, at least potentially, dangerous. Still, Haman has not said anything untrue. Then he goes on with his description, moving neatly from the difference of their laws to stating that they do not obey "the king's laws." It is only partly true that "their laws are different." Jews indeed had differences of dress, speech, diet, and so on. The appropriate word for this would be "customs" rather than "laws." None of these customs would violate the laws of the kingdom. Only Mordecai is known to have disobeyed one of the king's commands. Haman thus extends this one instance of disobedience to all the people. Then he quickly hammers home his main point, that the king should not tolerate such a situation. His request is straightforward, the need for subtlety gone, and he offers to pay for the effective destruction of this group that clearly threatens the kingdom.

The king, this manipulable and obtuse ruler, who is scared of losing control, is putty in the hands of his adviser. He gives Haman his ring, the powerful symbol of his authority. At this highly significant moment of bestowing even more power on Haman than he had already, Haman is once more identified. This time the text cites not only his ancestry but calls him "the enemy of the Jews" (v. 10). This is the only time that the word "Jews" occurs in this section. The king has given royal authority to one who is a deadly threat to the Jewish people by past allegiance and present disposition. This enemy of the Jews now has royal authority; now, by the king's words he can do as he wants. The words translated "The money is given to you" in verse 11 sound as if the king is returning Haman's offer of payment. More likely, the phrase means that the money promised by Haman is his to do with as he wishes, and so are the people. A more appropriate translation could be: "It's your money; deal with the people as you want."

The word "Jews" is not heard from the lips of either Haman or the king. Haman knows who the intended victims are, and the king's awareness is not needed. Race prejudice addresses people at the point of their fear. Haman's speech is a masterpiece of combining elements that raise Ahasuerus' fears. There are many of "them"; they are "different"; they set themselves against the laws of the land. Why, they will attempt a takeover soon! The same arguments that Haman uses can be found in a more explicit fashion in the Exodus story when Pharaoh convinces his people of the danger posed in their midst by the presence of the children of Israel (Exod. 1:9–10). Difference is the provoking element; the numbers aggravate the threat posed by this difference. Such prejudices can be heard as easily today as they were in the days of Haman.

The stakes are much higher this time than at the opening of the story. The king has become such a hands-off administrator that he lets his adviser wreak havoc in the realm. Hidden in the story is the threat that is now posed to queen Esther. The king, presumably, does not know her ethnic identity, nor that she is potentially a member of the people singled out for destruction. We, the readers, do know and are therefore also apprehensive on her behalf. Will another queen disappear?

A Decree in
Every Province (3:12–15)

All is now ready for the announcement of impending doom for the Jewish community. As before, the details of the process of issuing the decree are described meticulously, leaving the impression of a huge administrative apparatus set in motion to put the decision into effect. Secretaries write the letters, which go to all the satraps, governors over all the provinces, officials, and "every people in its own language" (v. 12). Haman is the one who is in charge, even though the edict goes out "in the name of King Ahasuerus." The words "all" and "every" are repeated in each verse except the last to emphasize the extent of the enterprise and its thoroughness.

The intention of the edict is spelled out in verse 13 as follows: "giving orders to destroy, to kill, and to annihilate all Jews, young and old, women and children, in one day, the thirteenth day of the twelfth month, which is the month of Adar, and to plunder their goods." Three verbs spell out the destruction, as if one would not be enough to describe the disaster. Different groups of the community are identified to make clear that no one will be spared, and permission is given to take their possessions as loot. To make the announcement so far ahead of time may seem odd, but the kingdom was large. It all would take time, and the side effect would be to put the Jews in fear of their lives for a good long period of time. For those of us who experienced the Second World War, all of this sounds ominously familiar. The intent of the Nazis was certainly identical to that of Haman. The Nazis too had a huge administrative apparatus to deal with the genocide of the Jewish community and profited from the plunder of their possessions.

At the time of Haman there were those who planned and those who cooperated with the plans of annihilation. In the Nazi era, too many Christian communities cooperated or were passive in the face of the persecution that went on in their midst. The truth is that the Church over centuries had participated in hatred of the Jewish community, often in active persecution, and itself had worked to prepare the seedbed that saw the dreadful harvest of the Holocaust. Insofar as all Christian communities bear responsibility for what happened, we need to repent of our past hostility and acts of violence toward the Jews. In addition, we must be alert to what survives in our midst of anti-Jewish attitudes and theologies. The history of the Church with its sister faith, Judaism, is not a happy one. The Holocaust teaches us where the plans of a Haman find their logical end.

Finally, the words and actions of Haman can be applied by extension to all groups that suffer from prejudice because they do not conform somehow to the majority. We may feel just as threatened as Haman did by those who do things differently. Difference in customs, appearance, and speech are not always as welcome in the midst of the Christian community as they could be. Dislike and fear grow sometimes unnoticed into hatred. Such inhospitality toward what does not conform to the standard set by the majority must be uncovered and changed, for we are aware that in the realm of God, unlike the realm of Ahasuerus, groups and individuals keep their uniqueness and talents.

The king and Haman are not inclined to introspection, and the chapter ends with sitting down "to drink" (v. 15), no doubt with the sense of a job well done. There is, according to verse 15, confusion in the city of Susa where the edict has also been proclaimed. The turmoil may indicate that a large number of Jews were present in the city. The reaction in the city is thus entirely different from that of the court.

At any event, the stage has now been set for the characters to take their places according to the roles assigned to them. Everyone is in place, and we have some idea of what their actions will be. The king will be in denial, Haman will do as he pleases with the money and the people, and Mordecai will protest. The only person we cannot be sure of is Esther. Will she continue as she has begun? What is happening to Esther anyway? The casting of the lot happened in the twelfth year of the king, which means that five years have passed without a word about her welfare. Is Mordecai still walking around and asking about her? Has she managed to keep her secret all this time? What was her reaction to the edict? The following episodes provide answers to some of our questions.

7. The Intercession of Esther
Esther 4—7

In these chapters Esther is persuaded by Mordecai to plead with the
king for her people, and she makes her intercession successfully. Chapter 4 is key to the development of events, for Esther is far from eager to
take on the commission with which Mordecai charges her. Finally she
agrees and goes to speak with the king (chap. 5). This first interchange
between the king and Esther results in a party given by Esther for both
the king and Haman. At this first party, Esther's cause remains hidden
from the king, for she merely invites the two men back for another dinner (5:1–8). Two interludes focus on Haman and Mordecai. We see
Haman in an intimate scene with family and friends. Out of his exchange with his wife arises the plan to erect a gallows for Mordecai, who
will meet his death thus before the rest of his people (5:9–14). While
Haman is planning to speak with the king about this, the king is planning to do something special for Mordecai, whose former service in the
matter of the two villainous eunuchs has just been recalled for him. The
king's desires and Haman's ambition are this time not in accord with
one another, and Haman is forced to see another receive the honors he
was hoping to get himself (6:1–11). This reversal bodes ill for Haman's
fate, as his friends and family foresee (6:13). The two interludes with
their comical overtones relax the tension created by Esther's withhold-
ing her request (chap. 5).

At her next dinner Esther reveals her concern and points an accus-
ing finger at Haman, who meets his end on the gallows he planned
for Mordecai (chap. 7). Esther and Mordecai are given Haman's former position and property. This episode solves individual difficulties
in a satisfactory way, but the Jews still need a resolution for their
predicament, as will become evident from the final section of the
book.

A CONVINCING ARGUMENT
Esther 4

In Sackcloth and Ashes (4:1–8)

4:1 **When Mordecai learned all that had been done, Mordecai tore his clothes and put on sackcloth and ashes, and went through the city, wailing with a loud and bitter cry;** [2] **he went up to the entrance of the king's gate, for no one might enter the king's gate clothed with sackcloth.** [3] **In every province, wherever the king's command and his decree came, there was great mourning among the Jews, with fasting and weeping and lamenting, and most of them lay in sackcloth and ashes.**

This chapter is full of comings and goings. Each episode has either Mordecai or Esther in the center. They remain in one place, while those who enable the communication, Esther's servants, move back and forth between them. Once more, the servants fulfill the crucial role of passing on information. The movement in the chapter anticipates the decisive movement that must be made by Esther in behalf of her people. There is a great deal of communication in the chapter; but, on the other hand, there is a great deal that is left unsaid, and a number of questions are raised that do not find easy answers. This has the effect of raising the level of tension for the reader.

First we meet Mordecai who, on learning the news, goes into ritual acts of mourning, tearing his clothes and wearing the garments of grief and humiliation, sackcloth and ashes. He does not go about this silently but makes a good deal of noise with his wailing over the fate that is to befall his people. Then he goes up to the entrance of the palace gate, since people in mourning garb are not allowed any further. The Jewish community joins in the activity of mourning everywhere. They fast, weep, and lament, and wear sackcloth and ashes also. Literally, the Hebrew states that they made their bed in sackcloth and ashes. Fasting and the wearing of ritual garments of humility may accompany mourning or repentance (2 Kings 18:37; Ezra 8:21, 23; Neh. 9:1; Jon. 3:8, for example). Traditionally, prayer would be a part of these rites, but neither Mordecai nor the community is said to pray. Instead of adding prayer in verse 3, the actions of weeping are repeated, with a different word, "lamenting." There seems to be an almost deliberate avoidance of the mention of a specific religious aspect.

Not all the reasons for Mordecai's behavior are self-evident. Sackcloth and ashes also point to repentance, and although it is clear that Mordecai is mourning, we wonder whether he is also repenting. Had he not counted on such an extreme reaction from Haman, and does he feel himself somewhat responsible in having set in motion such disastrous results of his disobedience? Further, although it is understandable that he grieves, why make such a display of it? And why does he go so close to the palace? Is he trying to draw attention to himself?

If drawing attention was his aim, he certainly succeeds, for Esther gets to hear of Mordecai's actions through her servants. Esther now moves back into the picture and will stay there most of the time until the end of the book. The text states that she became "deeply distressed" (v. 4). Why does Mordecai's behavior distress her so? Is it because she worries about him? Or is she worried that he will attract too much attention and their relationship and thus her secret will be revealed? The text leaves many of our questions unanswered, but it is clear that Esther returns to the story as a person who is afraid. Has she lived so long in fear of discovery that it has become a pattern of her daily life? The way in which Esther is introduced here does not raise the expectation of strong independent behavior.

First she sends Mordecai clothes (v. 4). She simply wants him to stop doing what he is doing. Only after he refuses the clothes does she send to find out what is going on. This action on Esther's part is revealing of her isolation. Apparently she does not know of the edict. She of all the Jews does not see the need to engage in acts of mourning. The harem has kept her from news that everyone else knows. Would her servants not have told her what was going on? Or had Esther not paid attention? Is she so focused on hiding that she has no use for news of the outside world, of her community? The servants who come and tell her about Mordecai must have known something of their relationship. Another possibility is that the servants were trying to protect her from knowledge that would only grieve her. There is something that all the world knows that Esther does not know; likewise, there is something all the world knows of which Mordecai is ignorant, as we will see. The worlds of these two people are quite apart from each other. In order for them to communicate, Esther must use the services of a servant, and the go-between in this episode is the eunuch "Hathach."

Mordecai gives Hathach all the information, supposedly including his refusal to do obeisance, for the text refers to "all that had happened to him" (v. 7). In addition, he knows about the money, "the exact sum," that Haman is willing to spend. Presumably, these details were not a part of the official edict, so Mordecai must have heard it elsewhere. Was it common knowledge, the way such things get around? Or did Mordecai have special information? We know from an earlier episode that he has his ear to the ground (2:19–21). The text does not reveal the source of Mordecai's knowledge. Next he hands Hathach a copy of the edict, of which there was most likely no scarcity. The paper serves to verify and authorize the words of Mordecai. The last part of verse 8 cuts abruptly into the more or less neutral territory of passing on the facts. Mordecai is apparently well aware that Esther does not know about the impending destruction of the Jews. The first thing that needs to be done then is to inform her in as thorough a fashion as possible. To this end he instructs Hathach and gives him the document. Only then does it become clear what the main purpose is of enlightening Esther. Mordecai wants Esther to make intercession for the Jews.

The verb for "charge" used in verse 8 is the same as the one that occurs in 2:10 and 2:20, where Esther is said to do as Mordecai "charged" her in terms of her identity. Mordecai, in line with patterns already established, now gives Esther another charge; this time she must plead with the king for her people. Mordecai is banking on the old relationship still being in place where he charged and Esther did as he charged her. His new charge, the plea for the Jewish people, means a reversal of the old one, which pertained to Esther's secrecy about her identity. This secret will of necessity have to be revealed if Esther takes on the new charge.

Esther's Refusal (4:9–11)

> 4:10 Then Esther spoke . . . [11] "All the king's servants and the people of the king's provinces know that if any man or woman goes to the king inside the inner court without being called, there is but one law—all alike are to be put to death. Only if the king holds out the golden scepter to someone, may that person live. I myself have not been called to come in to the king for thirty days."

The focus moves back to Esther, who hears the message from Mordecai via Hathach. Then the text, until now reporting only indirectly what people said, moves to quoting Esther's words directly. It is the first time that direct speech is assigned to Esther, and the direct references bring both her and her words into sharper focus. We begin to see things from Esther's perspective. What all the world knew about the Jews, Esther did not know, but there is something that everyone else knows that Mordecai does not know. The first part of her reply consists also of information. Esther's world is that of the court and more immediately that of the harem. Her life is circumscribed by the rules and customs that govern this place. Her world is confined and confining. Here, the master rules in his house, and without his invitation, his summons, no one is to approach him. Those who approach the king without an invitation are put to death, so explains Esther, unless the king holds out his scepter to them. Although nothing is known about such a law being operative in the Persian Empire, the truth is that King Ahasuerus has the power of life and death over Esther.

Then she adds information that is even more disturbing. She has not been called to go to the king in a month. The implication is that she does not expect the king to call again. Five years have passed, as we saw in the previous chapter, and Esther is moving to the background of the king's awareness. Her queenship is not a matter of any real power; like the other women, she must wait until she is invited. Did Mordecai not know this? It seems now that Mordecai has not been asking about her welfare as consistently as he once did, for surely he would have known such a fact. Or did he know, but did this information play no role in his charge to her?

Esther is, in any case, not of a mind to take on Mordecai's charge. She does not say outright that she will not go, but rather points to the risks if she follows his orders. She lives indeed by the laws of this kingdom, at peril of her life. And what good will she be to her people as a dead diplomat? The Esther who once did as Mordecai charged her, who obediently followed everyone's advice, is gone. Perhaps that person would not have served the task so well, for she will need her wits if she is to do her intercession successfully.

Mordecai's Reply (4:12–14)

> 4:13 Mordecai told them to reply to Esther, "Do not think that in the king's palace you will escape any more than all the other Jews. [14] For if you keep silence at such a time as this, relief and deliverance will rise for the Jews from another quarter, but you and your father's family will perish. Who knows? Perhaps you have come to royal dignity for just such a time as this."

Mordecai's words, like Esther's, are quoted directly. He issues a warning followed by a question. His speech goes straight to the heart of the matter. He does not say, as he could have done: "Your safety comes first, wait and see whether the king calls for you in another month." He does not tell her that she has obviously become an unsuitable candidate for mediation, and that they have to think of another plan. First he tells her not to think that she will get out alive while all others in her community die. She is as vulnerable as the rest of the Jews. It may even be that she will perish while the rest survive, if she keeps silent (v. 14). He closes with a question to the effect that she may well be where she is just for this purpose.

It is not a very diplomatic speech. Many people think that the term "another quarter" in verse 14 is a veiled reference to divine rescue. It is possible. On the other hand, we must be careful not to read religious references into the text just because we want them to be there. It is just as likely that Mordecai threatens human interference, in behalf of the Jews and against Esther. Basically, he points out to her that she has little to lose.

It is, paradoxically, Esther's silence that has worked *for* her until this time. Now she must break it, in behalf of her community, the very group from which she has been cut off. Twice Mordecai uses the term "such a time as this" (v. 14). It is a time of crisis; a time when disaster looms for the Jews; a time when Esther must make a decision.

The question "Who knows?" sets up strong echoes in the biblical text. It is used elsewhere to precede a reference to the possibility of God's gracious activity. So king David expresses his hope when his child is desperately ill: "Who knows? The LORD may be gracious to me, and the child may live?" (2 Sam. 12:22). In the book of Jonah, the king of Nineveh, in urging his people to repent, speculates on God's grace in this way: "Who knows? God may relent . . . " (see also Joel 2:14). The question "Who knows?" opens up the possibility of hope and liberation from distress with God as deliverer. Here the deliverer is human, all too human. Esther has been passive in the story so far, following the advice of the men in power around her, getting by on her beauty and charm. She is prudent, perhaps too much so. When her cousin and former guardian creates too much of a disturbance, she is afraid, and her first instincts are to stop him. Yet the words of Mordecai open up the possibility that "at a time such as this" she may well be the one to step forward.

Esther's Acceptance (4:15–17)

4:15 **Then Esther said in reply to Mordecai,** [16] **"Go, gather all the Jews to be found in Susa, and hold a fast on my behalf, and neither eat nor drink for three days, night or day. I and my maids will also fast as you do. After that I will go to the king, though it is against the law; and if I perish, I perish."** [17] **Mordecai then went away and did everything as Esther had ordered him.**

For the first time, the text omits mention of the ones who pass messages back and forth between Esther and Mordecai; it quotes Esther as if she is speaking directly to Mordecai. The person who was the go-between,

Hathach, who first appeared by name, has gradually faded out of the picture, with the vague and general "they" taking his place in verse 12. This device has the effect of pulling the two main characters more to the fore; in addition, the omission of the messenger emphasizes the urgency of the matter that is under discussion.

Esther issues a series of commands: "Go . . gather . . . hold a fast . . . neither eat nor drink" (v. 16). She is taking charge. No longer taking advice, asking questions, or explaining her situation, she puts herself in the position of telling Mordecai what to do next. To emphasize this reversal, she issues first her commands and then announces her decision. The Jews in the empire are already fasting, but Esther calls a fast for a different purpose than the one of bemoaning their fate. Like a soldier preparing for battle, she will fast together with her female entourage to prepare herself for her task (see Judg. 20:26; 1 Sam. 14:24; 2 Chron. 20:3). In so doing she obligates her community to join her, drawing them around her as a protective force. Symbolically, she breaks down the separation between herself and her people by asking them to fast for her. From now on she belongs to them and they to her; their fate will be her fate. This is the second time in the story that women are mentioned as engaging in action as a group; the first time of such activity was the women's party given by queen Vashti (1:9). Besides joining herself to her community, Esther calls on the solidarity of her women. Both groups betoken vulnerability in this realm; yet, in both cases Esther seeks her natural alliances. She identifies herself as a Jew and as a woman, together with other Jews and other women.

Again, there is no mention of prayer at a point where it would be most natural to include it. We may assume that prayer was a part of this fast, but it remains striking that the writer does not record it. The light is strongly focused on Esther as she orders her terse commands and announces her intention. She will go to the king in full knowledge of what she is about to do. It is "against the law," and she may die. Esther's earlier reluctance makes her decision all the more astonishing. Her words and Mordecai's reply, as recorded in verses 9–14, have revealed the reality of her situation and that of her community as one of peril for both. There is no more hiding now; she is who she is and will face the one who has the power of life and death over her in that knowledge. In the meantime she has taken charge of her life. There is a complete role reversal between her and Mordecai, who now follows all her instructions as she had once followed his.

What has convinced Esther to change her mind? Beyond revealing her initial reaction of distress to Mordecai's behavior in verse 4, the text does not report her feelings. We are left to infer them from her words. Somehow,

Mordecai's words have jolted her from passivity into activity, so she takes command of the situation. Was it the threat to her life that Mordecai pointed out, the thought that she has indeed nothing to lose, that persuades her to have a change of heart? Or was it the thought of the remote chance, the possibility, of success? It could be that the phrase "a time like this," used twice by Mordecai, had the greatest impact. Mordecai made clear that this is a time of great urgency. For Esther this is the moment of choice. Perhaps Mordecai's speech helped her see that "a time like this" also means an opportunity for her to become her own person. If we imagine ourselves in Esther's shoes, we may feel kinship with her efforts to make herself invisible, with her hesitancy to take on something that will imperil her life, and with her feelings of rejection in terms of her standing with the king. Mordecai presents her with a threat but also with a possibility. The threat is that she has very little to lose, for her life may be forfeit either way. The possibility is that she is in the harem for a purpose, a greater purpose than that of pleasing the king. It may take harsh words at times to jolt us out of our complacency and set us in a new direction.

Her words "if I perish, I perish" point to the realism that she has gained in this episode. It may well be that she will not be effective and will lose her life in the attempt. She knows now that this is a crisis situation. Beauty and charm alone will not get her what is needed this time. The survival of her community hangs by the slender thread of the "Who knows?"

ESTHER'S FIRST PARTY
Esther 5

Esther's Request (5:1–8)

> 5:1 On the third day Esther put on her royal robes and stood in the inner court of the king's palace, opposite the king's hall. The king was sitting on his royal throne inside the palace opposite the entrance to the palace. 2 As soon as the king saw Queen Esther standing in the court, she won his favor and he held out to her the golden scepter that was in his hand. Then Esther approached and touched the top of the scepter. 3 The king said to her, "What is it, Queen Esther? What is your request? It shall be given you, even to the half of my kingdom."

The tension raised by the end of the last chapter is quickly resolved in the first three verses of chapter 5. Esther cuts her fast somewhat short in order to make her first move—surviving an uninvited encounter with the

king. She goes while her community is still fasting in her behalf (4:16), that
is to say, with the full support of her people. Verse 1 places each of the two
main characters in their position: Esther *stands* outside of the king's hall;
the king *sits inside* the palace on his "royal throne." Esther waits outside,
standing, perhaps getting up her nerve to approach and speak to the king.
There is no mention of servants or maids, and we may imagine her to be
quite alone. She has put on her Sunday best, her "royal robes." The text
does not provide a reason. Did she dress up to give herself courage? To
enhance her charms and so convince the king? We may let our imagination play with the possibilities. Perhaps she wanted to be noticed as *queen*
and not just any woman from the harem. The king, in any case, is quick to
notice her, and as she once did with all who were in charge of her, she wins
the king's favor.

In contrast to Esther, the king is surrounded by symbols of his authority: the palace, the royal throne, the golden scepter (vv. 1–2). His power is
real and firm, represented by building, seat, and staff. He sits in the wealth
and splendor of his kingdom, ready to dole out life and death, while Esther
stands hesitantly, just in view. The king must make the first move or she
will indeed perish. Only when he holds out the scepter to her can she come
forward and touch it. Once Esther has been admitted into his presence, the
king behaves in a very friendly fashion, asking her what she wants and
promising up to half of his kingdom. The latter is not meant to be taken
literally, but indicates that he is willing to go to great lengths to satisfy her
desires. The king is so jovial, one almost suspects him of feeling a bit guilty.
Here he had almost forgotten the existence of the very one he made queen
in Vashti's stead! So he calls her "Queen Esther" (v. 3).

It is certainly a propitious moment for Esther to make her intercession.
To our surprise, she refrains from bringing up anything serious and invites
the king and his best friend and adviser, Haman, to come to dinner. A
strange turn of events! Did her courage fail her at the last minute? It is
more likely that she has designed her plans carefully. First the king has to
notice her; then she has to survive, and that is enough for the moment. We
know already that this king likes to eat and drink. Thus Esther follows the
king's questions and his offer of a gift with a gift of her own—a dinner invitation. It may seem ludicrous to us that anyone would risk one's life for
such a trivial matter. The king, who is not inclined to much reflection, responds with alacrity to Esther's request. Let's get Haman, he says, so that
"we may do as Esther desires" (v. 5).

We notice how the king who once banished a queen because she refused
his invitation is ready to bestow largesse on one who comes uninvited into

his presence. Ironically, this queen has an invitation of her own. At her banquet, the most important men of the kingdom will be entertained. In a role traditional for a woman, Esther will be hostess. Her designs are not traditional, but it is clear that she does everything to prevent suspicions from arising and to ward off one of the king's mood swings, from extravagant generosity to outrageous anger.

Once more, the king and Haman are drinking wine, and we expect that Esther will take advantage of the moment when the king asks her again what she desires (v. 6). It is almost irritating when Esther responds with a second invitation. Moreover, she builds up to this innocuous moment with elaborate prefatory phrases: "This is my petition and request: If I have won the king's favor, and if it pleases the king to grant my petition and fulfill my request . . . " (vv. 7–8). Only her last words give any indication that she has more on her mind than having fancy dinners prepared for Ahasuerus and Haman, and that her real petition is still waiting: "then I will do as the king has said" (v. 8).

The tension created by the exchange between Esther and Mordecai in chapter 4 is somewhat resolved, but new issues have arisen in this episode. Esther has, at least, survived her first and most chancy encounter with the king. Now it seems that she is waiting for the most opportune moment to take the next step. Even so, we wonder whether she is simply putting off her task. It seems also as if she has raised the stakes by inviting Haman to her dinners. Does this not jeopardize her and her community even more? Haman is, after all, the one who is the real schemer of the genocidal plan aimed at the Jews. Does she intend to lull his suspicions also? We are, in any case, still waiting to see a resolution of Esther's intercession when she issues her second invitation.

Haman at Home (5:9–14)

The next episode, together with chapter 6, functions as an interlude, humorous but with dark undertones. First, Haman, who has had a good time at the queen's table, hastens home to boast to his family what a fine fellow he is and how high his standing is with the king and now also with the queen (vv. 10–12). Before he arrives home, he encounters Mordecai, who does not move a muscle in front of Haman. The text makes it seem as if Mordecai ignored Haman: "he neither rose nor trembled before him" (v. 9). All this intimidation and no visible effect! When he recounts before his friends and family what a great and mighty person he really is, he ends with the observation that seeing Mordecai sitting at the king's gate spoils it all for him: "all this does me no good so long as I see the Jew Mordecai sitting at the king's gate" (v. 13).

Here is the tyrant with his self-inflated image in vivid colors. He gets his entourage together for the specific purpose of pointing out to them how great he is, even reminding them of the number of his sons; he has so much, he could hardly rise higher. There is just this one thing, the fact that Mordecai will not bow to him. If only he had that, his world would be all right. His surroundings are quick to point to an all too obvious solution. Although it would have been unwise to lay hands on Mordecai alone, and punitive measures for his entire people are certainly appropriate, at this point nothing stands in the way of executing Mordecai ahead of time. Surely, Haman will be able to convince the king of the merits of this idea. Such an advance execution will have the double effect of removing Mordecai's offending presence from Haman's world and of striking even more terror into the heart of the Jews.

Zeresh, Haman's wife, voices the plan together with his friends: "Let a gallows fifty cubits high be made, and in the morning tell the king to have Mordecai hanged on it; then go with the king to the banquet in good spirits" (v. 14). Fifty cubits amounts to 75 feet. A gallows of extraordinary proportions will be the only way to satisfy Haman's disproportionate reactions. It is most likely that a stake was used instead of a gallows, which creates an even more ferocious and off-putting image. Haman, however, sees no problems. In fact, he goes ahead and has the instrument of execution made even before he has the approval of the king. Just as once he had cast the lot to decide on the extermination of the Jews and then went to get royal approval, now he erects the gallows before he knows whether the king will let Mordecai hang from it. A huge gallows casting a huge shadow is the symbol of Haman overreaching himself.

What now of Esther's second dinner? Will Mordecai be dead by the time she is ready to make her mediation? Will it be too late for Mordecai? Has she waited too long? Such questions arise when the episode closes on a Haman who is as happy as he was when leaving the palace earlier: "This advice pleased Haman, and he had the gallows made" (v. 14).

Throughout the chapter Esther and Haman are portrayed in contrasting ways. Esther is not certain of her standing with the king. She waits for him to bridge the gap between them with the scepter and then proceeds to offer him something that she knows will please him. Moreover, her offer could not be less threatening and more in the tradition of what one can expect of her as a powerless woman. Although she stands in her royal robes, they do not betoken her power. She is a queen, but rules no people;

she is certainly not the queen of the Jews. Haman is her contrasting counterpart. Where her designs are for the salvation of the Jews, his plans are for their destruction. Where she acts modestly and extremely deferential, Haman brags and puffs himself up and loses his composure because one person refuses to show him deference. He will go to the king for approval of Mordecai's execution but sees this as mostly a *pro forma* matter, so he has the gallows made ahead of time. He loves being included in Esther's party, not knowing that Esther is one of the people for whom he has plotted extermination. His ignorance will cost him dearly, as we will see.

ROYAL HONORS
Esther 6

A Comedy of Errors (6:1–14)

> 6:6 So Haman came in, and the king said to him, "What shall be done for the man whom the king wishes to honor?" Haman said to himself, "Whom would the king wish to honor more than me?"

Chapter 6 continues the interlude, postponing the moment when Esther will face the king with her real petition. The scene is full of irony and pokes fun at the figures of power in the story, the king and Haman. It ends on a dark note, announcing Haman's impending downfall. In the opening verses 1–5, the king, perhaps from a surfeit of food and drink, has trouble falling asleep and asks for a reading. The records, or annals, may not sound to us like a fun bedtime story, but they contain, after all, some entertaining and, to the king, surprising news. When Ahasuerus hears the story of the two villainous eunuchs and their plot, and of Mordecai's role in the affair, he wants to know the reward that Mordecai received for his service. In chapter 2 the text stated explicitly that Esther "told the king in the name of Mordecai" (2:22). So we must assume that Ahasuerus had conveniently forgotten the entire event, including Mordecai's contribution and that he had not benefited in any way from his intervention. It was all a long time ago, and plots to assassinate the king may have been quite frequent. In any case, the king wants to do something now, being in a giving mood. As usual, he needs some help in figuring everything out and wants to know whether there is anyone around, presumably to give him advice. The servants, once again obliging with important information, tell him that Haman is around. "Just the man," thinks the king. The reader knows why Haman is on the scene, but the king has no idea, of course. He asks Haman what he thinks would be an appropriate reward for someone whom the king wishes to honor. Perhaps in order to have Haman render a truly objective judgment, Ahasuerus omits the name of Mordecai (v. 6).

Then the comedy of errors begins. Naturally, Haman believes the king to be referring to himself, and in great detail proposes just what he thinks such a person deserves: royal robes, a royal horse, and a royal crown; servants to attend to the honoree; and a public display of all this symbolic glory with a proclamation: "Thus shall it be done for the man whom the king wishes to honor" (v. 9). As the king had withheld the name of the potential recipient, so Haman keeps the names anonymous of those who will dance attendance on the one the king wishes to honor. He indicates only that it must be someone of high rank: "one of the king's most noble officials" (v. 9).

Verse 10 swiftly unravels Haman's delusions when the king identifies the one to be honored as Mordecai, and the one to do the honors as himself, Haman. The king's instructions keep the name of the recipient hidden as long as possible. First, Haman gets the news that he will be the one to make sure it all happens as he himself has instructed; thus Haman becomes aware that he cannot be the one the king wishes to honor. As soon as that part of the bad news has penetrated, the blow falls: "do so to the Jew Mordecai" (v. 10). "So Haman took the robes and the horse and robed Mordecai and led him riding through the open square of the city, proclaiming, 'Thus shall it be done for the man whom the king wishes to honor'" (v. 11). Haman was caught in his own trap and now must walk around with the one who refused to bow before him, elevated on a royal horse, while he must be the announcer of this good fortune. The honors are visible to all, for they take place in the "open square," by Haman's own directions.

In contrast to this emphasis on public exposure, Haman and the king operate with obtuseness in this episode, and we may see the darkness of nighttime as symbolic for their ignorance and lack of insight. Haman has come to the court to discuss Mordecai's execution, of which he is so confident that the gallows is already put up. He is ignorant of the important service that Mordecai once did for the king and of the story of Bigthana and Teresh. In the end, Mordecai, the star recipient of the king's favor, is elevated on a horse rather than a gallows, and Haman the executioner becomes Haman the proclaimer of good news for Mordecai. The gallows is standing empty, ready to receive its victim. The gallows does not care who hangs from it.

The king is first ignorant of Mordecai's service, and, once he is enlightened as to that matter, he is not aware of Haman's designs. His part in the conversation consists mostly of questions: "what?" "who?" and "how?" He seems unable to think things out for himself. He refers to Mordecai as a Jew without making the connection between Mordecai and the community for which he has ordered extermination, and the imminent destruction of which he and his trusted adviser, Haman, have celebrated over drinks not long before (3:15). The most logical reward for Mordecai would have been to safeguard his life.

Mordecai has no speaking part in the episode. He may have been as taken aback as Haman when he turns out to be the one to ride around in royal splendor in the sight of all. He was perhaps gratified with his own elevation and his enemy's humiliation but in the end must also have known that this parade in itself solves nothing for him or his community.

In the last section of the chapter, the shadows that are falling over Haman's life are becoming more ominous (vv. 12–14). First Haman goes home in mourning, a total contrast to his earlier good spirits. He tells his friends and wife all that has befallen him, and his entourage responds to the revelations with a dire warning: "His advisers and his wife Zeresh said to him, 'If Mordecai, before whom your downfall has begun, is of the Jewish people, you will not prevail against him, but will surely fall before him'" (v. 13). Here is no attempt to cheer up one's poor husband and friend, no effort to make him feel better. Their words contain the root for the verb "fall" three times in Hebrew and read literally: "if from the seed of the Jews is Mordecai before whom you have begun to fall, you will not prevail over him, but will fall, yes fall, before him." Ironically, the Jews are portrayed as a threat rather than as victims. The one who should have fallen before Haman, Mordecai, has not fallen but is raised in honor instead, and now it will be Haman who will fall. These are not words to make anyone feel more optimistic. They are put into the mouths of Haman's intimates, with a sense of heavy irony. Surely, everyone knows by now that Mordecai is a Jew, and it is clear from a previous episode that Haman's family knew. This fact does not need to be called into question (5:13–14). Surely, no wife would speak so to her husband when he is down, and no friend would give this sort of advice. The writer portrays Haman's family as taking a healthy distance in advance from this man who will go to the palace next to meet his doom.

The time has come for the queen's dinner party, and the eunuchs are at the door to escort Haman. The tempo of the story is now speeding up, indicated by the quick succession of verbs and the emphasis on haste; they "hurried Haman off" (v. 14).

ESTHER'S SECOND PARTY
Esther 7

A Question of Life (7:1–6)

7:3 Then Queen Esther answered, "If I have won your favor, O king, and if it pleases the king, let my life be given me—that is my petition—and the lives of my people—that is my request. [4] For we have been sold, I and my people, to be destroyed, to be killed, and to be annihilated. If we had been sold merely as slaves, men and women, I would have held my peace; but no enemy can compensate for this damage to the king." [5] Then King Ahasuerus said to Queen Esther, "Who is he, and where is he, who has presumed to do this?" [6] Esther said, "A foe and enemy, this wicked Haman!" Then Haman was terrified before the king and the queen.

The text no longer dwells on details but moves quickly to the second day of the banquet when the king once more invites Esther to make her petition (7:1–2). The fact that there was a second day to the banquet indicates that this was no minor dinner but an extensive event with extensive drinking. The king repeats his earlier invitation almost word for word. The only variation is that he addresses Esther by her title, as he had done when she first appeared before him as uninvited intercessor (5:3). In fact, in this episode Esther is referred to as Queen Esther throughout, or as the queen (see vv. 6 and 8). Whereas in earlier episodes her title occurred only rarely, its addition in this passage serves to highlight her status and dignity.

This time, she does not hold back but lays her request before the king. She precedes her petition with the obligatory polite phrases and then goes straight to the heart of the matter, begging for her life and that of her people. She points out that it is indeed a matter of life and death, repeating three different verbs for destruction, in fact, repeating the words of the edict itself (3:13). Her speech is relatively long, the longest speech Esther has made so far. In underlining the desperation of the situation, she adds that she would not have bothered the king if it had been merely a matter of being sold into servitude. The very last words of her speech are not clear, indicative perhaps that she did get tangled up in her argument. It could be that we should read "it would not have been proper to bother the king with such an injury" for the last part of verse 4. The moment toward which she has been preparing has arrived, and Esther must be as succinct, as clear, and as polite as possible. She manages the first and the last requirements, but not entirely the second one. Yet her reference to the threat on her life is clear enough and succeeds in getting the king's attention.

Esther has already made a choice for life when she chose to make intercession for her people. Her choice moved her out of a passive, secretive existence that amounted to a kind of death into an active, open, and resistant position, against death and for life. Ahasuerus' decision cannot take this away from her. In choosing for her own life, she chooses at the same time for her community. At this moment, Esther completes the bridging of the separation she once created between herself and her community at Mordecai's behest. Her safety and the safety of the Jews are not separate matters. Prudently, she mentions herself first to draw the king's interest. In verse 4 she continues her plea in the first person plural, "we have been sold." What began symbolically by the communal fast now finds concrete expression. Whereas in 4:16, Esther referred to her community as "all the Jews," here she names them "my people."

Ahasuerus is not interested, however, in the identity of the people, but in the culprit who is behind the plan for destruction. His response to Esther's petition takes the form of questions, his habitual mode of speaking, since he needs assistance in obtaining necessary information most of the time. He wants to know who is behind this scheme; he apparently hadn't paid much attention to his giving Haman authority for this very purpose and to the words of the edict that went out in his name. He sounds properly indignant, and Esther is not one to let the grass grow under her feet at this time. She points her finger directly at Haman, identifying him twice as an adversary and calling him wicked. Naturally, this has Haman terrified, as anyone in his shoes would be.

Haman's Fall (7:7–10)

The king has become so overwhelmed by anger that he needs to take a stroll, time to cool off (v. 7). In the meantime, Haman makes his last and fatal move by throwing himself on the mercy of the queen. He literally falls on the couch where she lies, continuing his fall foretold in his household, and there the returning king finds him. The king then accuses him, with deliberate or coincidental obtuseness, of accosting the queen (v. 8). This very accusation becomes the immediate motivation for Haman's execution. In contrast to Esther, who begs for her life successfully, Haman's attempt to beg for his life is interpreted as aggressiveness by the king. There is, fortunately, or unfortunately from Haman's point of view, a gallows ready. The servants are again ready to move matters along by providing useful information, and the king decides without further deliberation that Haman must hang from the gallows that he erected for Mordecai (vv. 9–10).

Haman's presence at Esther's dinner is thus essential for a partial solution to the problem posed by the story. Without Haman's clumsy attempt to arouse Esther's compassion, the king might not have had such a handy excuse to get rid of Haman. That Haman turns to Esther is somewhat strange, for on the face of it the king would seem to be a safer bet for him than Esther. Esther is a member of the Jewish people, and she has exposed him. Is Haman counting on a "woman's soft heart"? Such a stereotypical misinterpretation of Esther's "feminine nature" would lend a fine touch to Haman's final mistake.

Many interpreters of the Bible judge Esther harshly for her lack of compassion toward Haman, but the text leaves ambiguous what Esther would have done, for the king arrives before she can react. It is true that she does not contradict the king's interpretation of Haman's behavior. The story is not so much concerned with compassion but rather with the survival of those who live by their wit and prudent planning in spite of their vulnerable position, and the downfall of the powerful who have laid traps for them. Haman's downfall satisfies the reader's sense of poetic justice: The wicked schemer who would have had Mordecai swing from the highest gallows ever made has been caught by the very noose he had created. In throwing himself on Esther's mercy, he makes a fatal miscalculation. She, after all, is a member of the community he wants to destroy. It is not clear whether Haman has understood this fact from her petition. Perhaps he had dozed off earlier and heard only Esther's accusatory words that applied to him.

The king takes no responsibility at all for any of the schemes of Haman. The king is the one who condemns Haman to death. The king expresses no regret for his own participation in the plan to exterminate the Jews that would have included the queen. It is also possible that Ahasuerus is still partly unaware and does not know that the Jews are the targeted group or that Esther is Jewish and thus a member of this group.

The solution provided by Haman's death is indeed only a partial one. Esther's request for her life and that of her people has not received a response from the king. Haman's demise may guarantee Esther's safety, but her community is still far from safe. The pogrom will take place as long as the machinery that has been set in motion for it is not stopped. Esther's work is not yet done.

8. From Sorrow into Gladness
Esther 8—10

The Jewish community is the focus of concern in this last part of the story. In the final chapters the remaining difficulty of the immutable decree once issued for the destruction of the Jews is resolved by Esther's making another petition. The way out of the impasse is to allow the Jews to defend themselves against violent aggression. Esther and Mordecai have moved into powerful positions and become the main designers and executors of the countermanding orders (chap. 8). Chapter 9 describes in detail the destruction wrought by the Jews on their enemies. Esther makes one last petition to extend the violence into a second day inside the city. The last half of this chapter is devoted to a recapitulation of the main events of the book and the inauguration of the feast of Purim. A brief appendix, which highlights the position and stature of Mordecai, lacks any reference to Esther (10:1–3).

A HARVEST OF DESTRUCTION
Esther 8

Positions of Power (8:1–2)

First, the text makes sure to record the powerful positions taken by Esther and Mordecai. Esther inherits Haman's house and Mordecai the ring that the king had once bestowed on Haman. Also, Mordecai receives the oversight over Haman's estate from Esther. Esther is the powerful mover of events, telling the king of her relation to Mordecai (8:1). This short section resounds with the names of Esther and Mordecai, who are each mentioned three times in the span of two verses. Haman is also mentioned three times; he may be dead, but the evil he designed is alive and well, and the seeds of destruction sown by him are waiting in fertile ground to grow into a harvest.

Both Esther and Mordecai are very much alive and established in positions of power, but their people are still awaiting their deliverance. It may have been tempting for these two to refrain from further action. In their shoes, we might have called it a day. They have done what they could and achieved a great success; why not stop while they are ahead?

An Irrevocable Decree (8:3–14)

8:5 Esther rose and stood before the king. She said, "If it pleases the king, and if I have won his favor, and if the thing seems right before the king, and I have his approval, let an order be written to revoke the letters devised by Haman son of Hammedatha the Agagite, which he wrote giving orders to destroy the Jews who are in all the provinces of the king. 6 For how can I bear to see the calamity that is coming on my people? Or how can I bear to see the destruction of my kindred?"

The last step to be taken by Esther may have been the most difficult one. Unlike the previous occasions, she engages in a position of pleading (v. 3). Tears have not been a part of her intercession up until now. "The evil design" of Haman is, however, still in place and must somehow be averted. There is no mention this time of the danger of coming into the presence of the king uninvited. Has Esther become so powerful that this is no longer an issue for her? It is possible. Nevertheless, she withholds speaking until the king holds out the golden scepter (v. 4).

Her language is even more extravagantly polite than before, stringing four expressions of deference together before she issues her request. She asks for an order to revoke the plan of Haman, to whom she refers together with his descendance. The emphatic reference to Haman may have served to avoid any idea the king might have had that Esther holds him accountable for the edict that had been issued in his name. She ends her plea with a double question referring to her pain as a possible witness to the annihilation of her people, whom she finally calls "my kindred" (v. 6), sealing the identification between herself and her community. To indicate the focus of concern, the word "Jews" occurs with great frequency in this chapter. Esther moves from referring to them as "the Jews," to "my people," and last, to "my kindred." In contrast, explicit references to the Jews are absent from chapter 7 and from Esther's petition made in that chapter.

In his reply the king sounds both a little tired and helpless, as if he feels he has done enough and Esther should stop bothering him (vv. 7–8). Esther has all that Haman once had, and Haman has been punished. There is nothing more that he can do, since an irrevocable decree cannot be changed. To indicate his goodwill, perhaps, he does give permission for Esther and Mordecai to write a new edict if they can devise one. He gives them no advice and no encouragement. Esther and Mordecai have now fully taken Haman's place, with the king's handing to them the power to do as they "please" (v. 8). The last words of the king carry a double meaning. Because a royal edict cannot be revoked, the earlier decree for the pogrom cannot simply be undone. On the other hand, whatever edict Esther and Mordecai devise cannot be revoked either. It will depend on their cleverness whether they can effectively undo the first decision by their "irrevocable" decree.

Mordecai is with Esther, apparently, for the king addresses both of them in verses 7–8. Yet nowhere does he in his turn speak to the king himself. Esther does all the work of intercession. Mordecai's role comes into play with the issuing of the new edict in verses 9–14, which in places echo verbally the unfolding of events in 3:9–15, to allow the exact role reversals to play themselves out. In verse 9 the Jews are added as recipients of Mordecai's letters. Besides the obvious need to send the information to the pertinent group, the fact that the letters are also addressed to "the Jews" indicates that they are becoming a more viable section of the populace, having a voice in their own fate (v. 9). The upshot of the new decree is that the Jews are allowed by king's order to "defend their lives." (v. 11). The words used for their defense are identical to the earlier references to their own demise: "to destroy, to kill, and to annihilate" (3:13). This is the only way to upset the irrevocable edict issued earlier. Because both edicts are irrevocable, we may imagine more an armed struggle than an assault on unarmed people. We keep in mind the fictional character of the story, especially at this point. Esther is a Brer Rabbit tale of the stereotypically weak trickster who outwits all those in power and thus saves the lives of the vulnerable ones.

There is also a dark side to the reversal of victims and oppressors. One of the most devastating results of the violence of war and oppression is that it sets in motion counterviolence, the oppressed thus turning into a mirror image of the former oppressors. The greatest evil that "wicked Hamans" perpetrate may well be the lasting hatred between former victims and oppressors. The persecutions and attempts at annihilation of the Jews over the centuries inside Christian lands played a large role in the birth of the modern nation of Israel. The violence that we see sometimes perpetuated by Israel is the product of the violence perpetrated on the Jews especially during the Second World War. This recognition does not allow a blanket condoning of everything that happens in the state of Israel. Yet such insight sets the tone for repentance and understanding with which any statement about Israel from the Christian community must be prefaced.

Reactions in City and Province (8:15–17)

A last scene highlights Mordecai in his royal robes in contrast to his earlier sackcloth and ashes (4:1). The city of Susa is rejoicing, in contrast to the confusion it showed to the previous edict (3:15). And in the provinces and entire country, the Jews exhibit "gladness and joy," twice mentioned, in contrast to their earlier mourning and lamenting (4:3). Verse 17 adds a comical note, for "many of the peoples . . . professed to be Jews, because the fear of the Jews had fallen upon them," a reaction that is repeated twice in the next chapter (9:2–3).

If we recall the historic circumstances under which the story of Esther found its shape, the reference to "the fear of the Jews" sounds highly ironic. At no period during this time of subjection to large powers could the Jews be viewed realistically as a threat. The Jews were an ethnic minority among many minorities, in a small province of Persia, and as such were not likely to cause much fear anywhere. In such circumstances it may, on the other hand, be tempting to dream of possibilities where power brokers become victims and victims become warriors. Imagine! Instead of the Jews having to identify themselves as marked for destruction, by wearing their insignia as they had to do during the Hitler years, people flock to their ranks and want to be identified as Jews!

A DAY OF FEASTING AND GLADNESS
Esther 9:1–19

This chapter is full of references to "the Jews," thus making the events ring with the echoes of their identity. Former victims have become warriors because "on the very day when the enemies of the Jews hoped to gain power over them, but which had been changed to a day when the Jews would gain power over their foes, the Jews gathered in their cities throughout all the provinces of king Ahasuerus to lay hands on those who had sought their ruin" (9:1–2). In the end, 75,000 are reported killed (9:16).

Even if we take the fictional character of the story seriously, this part of the narrative may disturb us. There is no way to solve the obstacle posed to our sympathies by the unpleasant spectacle of this slaughter. But then, the intent of the story was not and is not to inspire sympathy for one group or another. Rather, the narrative aims to empower those who are beaten down with the incredible hope that their day will come. No amount of exaggeration is therefore left out: The Jews are powerful; Mordecai outshines everyone in fame and prestige (9:4); the Jews "did as they pleased to those who hated them" (9:5). Nothing is done to modify the bloodthirstiness of those who were destined for destruction. The administrative apparatus is now on the side of the Jews, apparently out of fear of Mordecai (9:3). The king, in a final appearance of total silliness, is pleased with the results—the destruction of a large number of his own people!—and asks whether there is anything else Esther wants (v. 12). She then makes her last request, which amounts to allowing the Jews a free hand for a second day (v. 13). She also asks for the death of Haman's sons, or for their dead bodies to be displayed on the gallows, if we follow the thread of narration in which they have already been killed (vv. 7–9).

It is possible that this twice-told demise of the sons of Haman points to two stories that are woven together: one with Mordecai and one with Esther in the center. The focus in these last chapters seems to switch from Esther to Mordecai and back again. Frequently one of them is on the scene without the other, especially when the focus is on Mordecai. At times one duplicates the actions of the other, as in the case of Haman's sons. Some scholars believe that there was an earlier story of one Mordecai who was a courtier at the court of Xerxes. The writer of the book of Esther would then have used this material to integrate it with a story that revolved around Esther. Such a process would explain the absence of Esther from the very last verses of the book, for example.

Gradually, the emphasis of the story shifts to the celebration of Purim, a celebration of Jewish survival against the odds. This feast showed some variety in its customs, a variety that is partly explained by Esther's request for the killing to continue a second day. Three times the text notes that the Jews took no property: "they did not touch the plunder" (vv. 10, 15, 16). That is to say that greed did not play a role in the actions of the Jews. This stands in contrast to the edict that had instructed their enemies to "plunder their goods" (3:13). *Purim* is a feast of triumph and also of generosity: "a holiday on which they send gifts of food to one another" (9:19).

PRACTICES OF PURIM
Esther 9:20—10:3

Gifts to the Poor (9:20–23)

In this section Mordecai is portrayed as the central figure who decrees the days of feasting, when they are to be held, how long they shall last, and what shall be done on them. Mordecai's directives frame the passage, to indicate the important role he played in establishing the festival: "Mordecai recorded these things, and sent letters to all the Jews. . . . So the Jews adopted as a custom what they had begun to do, as Mordecai had written to them" (9:20, 23). Although the recorded bloodshed that gave rise to the feast may be disturbing, we might think of the Fourth of July as a similar, albeit secular, celebration. The practices of Purim are not to continue to take revenge on the enemy; rather, they include a sharing of gifts and especially a giving of presents to the poor. Gratitude is used as a motivation for generosity.

These Days Are Called
Purim (9:24–10:3)

> 9:25 But when Esther came before the king, he gave orders in writing that the wicked plot that he had devised against the Jews should come upon his own head, and that he and his sons should be hanged on the gallows. [26] Therefore these days are called Purim, from the word Pur.

Esther moves back into the center as both the one who averted the impending disaster for the Jews and the one who joins Mordecai in ordering the feast of Purim. Verse 25 in Hebrew reads literally: "She came before the king," reading the feminine pronoun "she" where our English translation inserts Esther. In the Hebrew reading, the femaleness of the intercessor is stressed by the use of the pronoun. "She" is originally the most unlikely character in the story to accomplish deliverance of any sort. "She" is the one who hid in the shadows, cut off from her community. "She" is the alien, the orphan, the woman who unexpectedly stepped out of her corner to approach the one with power, in behalf of her people. Upon her intercession, Haman's evil plan was turned around to come down upon his own head. Esther counterplanned the evil plan of Haman. The feast is called the feast of "chance," Purim; yet it was not chance that saved the people, but Esther's clever, patient, and persistent mediation.

The appendix that draws Mordecai back into the center does not overshadow the importance of Esther (10:1–3). Perhaps the storyteller felt an obligation to return to the original story and Mordecai's virtues. Perhaps he felt that Esther's act needed to be balanced by a male display of power. Whatever the case may be, in one sense both Esther and Mordecai take a backseat to the community in these last chapters.

The feast at the end, a feast of survival, a people's celebration, stands in contrast to the opening feast of King Ahasuerus. That party, in which splendor and ostentation were at the center, was one that went on too long.

It was a feast, moreover, that ended in a woman's banishment. The last feast of the story, Purim, begins with bloodshed. Yet this party, unlike that of chapter 1, is one of people with one another. People give one another gifts; those who are not well off especially benefit. On a woman's intercession and by a woman's guidance the customs of Purim are established. A woman would not come into the king's presence when invited, and disaster followed. A woman came to the king uninvited, and events took a turn so that the tale ends with the sounds of laughter and the fireworks of rejoicing.

For Further Reading

Ezra-Nehemiah

Alberz, Rainer. *A History of Israelite Religion in the Old Testament Period.* Vol. 2: *From the Exile to the Maccabees.* Louisville, Ky.: Westminster John Knox Press, 1994.

Eskenazi, Tamara Cohn. *In An Age of Prose: A Literary Approach to Ezra-Nehemiah.* Society of Biblical Literature Monograph Series 36. Atlanta: Scholars Press, 1988.

Myers, Jacob M. *Ezra. Nehemiah.* The Anchor Bible. New York: Doubleday, 1965.

Esther

Moore, Carey A. *Esther.* New York: Doubleday, 1971.

Pfisterer Darr, Katheryn. *Far More Precious Than Jewels: Perspectives on Biblical Women.* Louisville, Ky.: Westminster John Knox Press, 1991.

van Wijk-Bos, Johanna W.H. *Ruth. Esther. Jonah.* The Knox Preaching Guides. John H. Hayes, ed. Atlanta: John Knox Press, 1986.

Weems, Renita. *Just a Sister Away: A Womanist Vision of Women's Relationships in the Bible.* San Diego: Luramedia, 1988.